PREPARED
NOT SCARED
COOKBOOK

PREPARED NOT SCARED COOKBOOK

WHAT TO STORE AND HOW TO FEED YOUR FAMILY FOR 5 WEEKS

LAURA ROBINS

GIBBS SMITH
TO ENRICH AND INSPIRE HUMANKIND

First Edition published 2006 as *Pantry Cooking*
Revised edition published 2020
24 23 22 21 20   6 5 4 3 2

Published by
Gibbs Smith, Publisher
P.O. Box 667
Layton, Utah 84041

Orders: 1.800.748.5439
www.gibbs-smith.com

Cover design by Virginia Brimhall Snow
Interior design by Sheryl Dickert
Printed and bound in USA
Library of Congress Cataloging-in-Publication Data

Robins, Laura.
  Pantry cooking: quick and easy food storage recipes / Laura Robins.—1st ed.
    p.cm.
  1. Quick and easy cookery. 2. Food—Storage. I. Title.
TX833.5.R62 2006
641.5'55—dc22
                    2006007036

ISBN: 978 1-4236-5676-0

This book is dedicated to my best friend, soulmate and husband, Thomas Frank Robins. The path in life that we share has lead to this work. Without his knowledge, support and encouragement, it would not be possible.

And to my children, Brittany Mariah Sutton, Beau John Frederick Robins, and Christian Dane Thomas Robins, thank you for giving me the reason to be more than I am.

And to my granddaughter, Sedona Skye Sutton, thank you for all of the joy.

Contents

Acknowledgments

I would like to thank all those who have taught and inspired me along the way while creating this book. I would also like to express my gratitude to Gibbs Smith, Publisher, for believing in my ideas and giving me this opportunity; thanks to my editor, Melissa Barlow, for her help and patience.

Introduction

I t is my hope that this book will not only help you to realize the importance of having a store of food, but inspire and motivate you to create a practical and convenient menu of meals that will not only save you time and money, but give you peace of mind.

WHY STORE FOOD?

What we learn from yesterday helps us to live adequately today by making preparations for tomorrow. To be responsible for ourselves (and our actions) should be foremost in the mind of everyone. Every parent hopes their child will become an independent and self-sufficient adult. Personal preparedness in health, education, finances and means such as the storage of food and water are not only attributes for the success of an individual, but for the family unit as well as the community as a whole. Even if we never need to live off our own store of food and water, we will have the ability to help our extended families, friends and neighbors in the event of a recession, job loss, bankruptcy, accident, illness, hurricane, earthquake, tornado, volcanic eruption, tsunami, act of terrorism, war or death. Natural disasters have occurred throughout history but seem to impact us more today because there are simply more people to take care of than ever before.

The first line of defense for our National Homeland Security is in the citizens' preparedness at home. Emergency responders, whether police, fire department, military personnel or citizen volunteers are better mentally suited to help deal with any disaster situation if they know that their own family is secure at home. A store of food and water is the foundation of that security and can provide peace of mind.

Wants vs. Needs

Once upon a time we were taught to set aside some of our earnings for "a rainy day." Today, in this society, we generally don't save for the things we want or need. We have been taught instant gratification by the vast amount of credit available to us. Between the never-ending rise in the cost of living and living beyond our means, each day we find ourselves deeper in debt. We have become slaves to this system.

Learn to recognize the difference between your own personal wants and needs. Educate yourself on what the most important basic survival elements are: attitude, air, shelter, fire, water and food. You can be doomed in a few seconds if you let fear and panic rule. You cannot live more than a few minutes without air. You cannot live more than a few hours in extreme temperatures without shelter or fire. You cannot live more than a few days without water and you will need food within a few weeks. These are needs. Almost everything else is a want.

Invest in Food!

In times of need, from the loss of a job to a catastrophic disaster, a store of food and water is priceless. We cannot eat or drink money, gold, diamonds or real estate investments!

Food is a very good investment. Acquiring food storage is a significant financial commitment. Make the necessary changes in spending habits to get out of debt. Spend less than you earn, not more. Limit food shopping trips to once a week. Use a shopping list to control spending and stop impulse-buying.

Date and price the items you are buying using a black permanent marker. This helps with rotation and enables you to track the rising cost of food and realize the value of your investment.

Whole Grains, the Cornerstone of Food Storage

All of the flour used in these recipes is freshly milled whole wheat or whole grain flour. Whole grains should be one of the first items considered for storage because it is inexpensive, versatile, and has a 20-year plus shelf life if stored under cool conditions in dry, air-tight containers. The tremendous benefit of freshly milling whole grains as it is needed is the presence of all of the nutrition it has to offer. If you purchase milled flour, it is virtually void of all nutrients after 30 days. An electric grain mill should be the next item to acquire because you need it to unlock any grain's fresh, nutritious flour and it only takes a couple of minutes to do it. It is also a good investment to purchase a hand-cranked grain mill for back-up, just in case you are without electricity for an extended period of time. The price of a good electric grain mill can be anywhere from approximately $170 to $400. A good manual, hand-cranked grain mill can cost from $90 to $600. There are also electric grain mills available with the option of disengaging the motor to become manual if needed. Some cost around $400. There are many good grain mill manufacturers, and many of them are listed in the Resources section on page 137.

STORE MEALS
The 5-Week Example Menu

It is difficult to make practical and convenient use out of following a vague food storage plan with hundreds of pounds of this-and-that per person. It's very abstract to deal with all of this bulk food without a specific way to incorporate it into everyday eating. Unfortunately, many sincere attempts at acquiring food storage have lead to throwing away many pounds of unused, forgotten, and un-rotated food. Storing what you actually do eat will save you a lot of money, time and effort.

Instead of storing food, think about storing meals!

The 5-Week Example Menu consists of meals that can be eaten off the shelf without electricity. Therefore, nothing fresh (other than sprouts), refrigerated or frozen is included in the recipes and they can also be easily and quickly prepared by alternative cooking methods. This menu of food storage meals is to be used as an example, a guide and a direction to follow when creating your own personalized menu for you and your family.

Basic and familiar meals were targeted in the selection of these storage recipes on the 5-Week Example Menu to provide a large variety of different ingredients and tastes with adequate nutrition and ease of preparation. When fresh fruit is unavailable, be sure to add at least two to three servings of canned or dried fruit to serve with your meals each week. For meals with recipes that have little or no vegetables in them, add canned vegetables such as stewed tomatoes, asparagus, 3-bean salad, refried beans, salsa, wild rice cakes, etc. on the side. Several recipes used in the 5-Week Example menu require little or no adaptation from the basic fresh recipe. Most of the ingredients are used every day in countless recipes under normal circumstances.

Many of the meals you prepare and eat on a regular basis have some canned or dried ingredients already in the recipes. These meals can easily be adapted to a recipe using only pre-cooked, canned and dried foods. It is important to experiment with adapting your favorite meals to find the ones that work best and taste good to you.

The rotation of the food storage is very important. It needs to be replenished consistently. It is important to always store the newly acquired item behind the older ones on the shelf. With all of these food storage meals made from only canned and dried foods (with the exception of sprouts), there is no way we would want to eat only this way every day with so much fresh, frozen or refrigerated food available to us! There are several ways to incorporate the food storage meals into our current and abundant lifestyle: use them occasionally as they are pre-cooked and completely off the shelf for fast, convenient meals that can be prepared in 30 minutes, or use some of the storage ingredients along with fresh ingredients for any recipe.

5-WEEK EXAMPLE MENU

Week 1	BREAKFAST	LUNCH	DINNER
SUNDAY	Swedish Pancakes	Tuna Salad Wrap with Sprouts	Chicken & Dumplings Fruit Cocktail
MONDAY	Corned Beef Hash & Eggs Toast	Franks & Beans, Bread, Applesauce	Fried Ham & Sweet Potatoes Creamed Corn Green Beans
TUESDAY	Oatmeal	Peanut Butter Surprise Sandwich	Red Beans & Rice Apple Crisp
WEDNESDAY	Mushroom Omelets Hash Browns Toast	Turkey Salad Sandwich with Sprouts	Spaghetti with Meat Sauce Crostini
THURSDAY	French Toast	Broccoli-Cheese Soup	White Chili with Chicken Tortillas Pineapple Rings
FRIDAY	Cream of Wheat	Macaroni & Cheese	Clam Chowder Hardtack Orange Slices
SATURDAY	Spam & Eggs Hash Browns Toast	Pinto Beans, Tortillas & Salsa	Beef Stroganoff Asparagus Cookies

Week 2	BREAKFAST	LUNCH	DINNER
SUNDAY	Salsa Omelets Hash Browns Toast	Ham Salad Sandwich with Sprouts	Turkey & Gravy Dressing Mashed Potatoes Green Beans Cranberry Sauce
MONDAY	Biscuits & Gravy	Sloppy Joes	Egg Foo Yung Pork Fried Rice with Peas & Carrots
TUESDAY	Pancakes	Bean & Cheese Burrito	Fettuccine with Capers, Black Olives & Tomatoes Peach Crumble
WEDNESDAY	Egg Sandwich	Split Pea Soup with Spam	Tacos with Ground Beef Refried Beans Salsa
THURSDAY	Oatmeal	Peanut Butter Surprise Roll Up	Green Chile, Chicken & Cheese Enchiladas
FRIDAY	French Toast	Tuna Salad Sandwich with Spouts	Smoked Salmon Cakes Stewed Tomatoes Fruit Cocktail
SATURDAY	Grits	Tomato Soup Cheese Sandwich	Irish Stew Colcannon Brownies

Week 3	BREAKFAST	LUNCH	DINNER
SUNDAY	Swedish Pancakes	Franks & Beans Bread Applesauce	Chicken Couscous 3-Bean Salad Vanilla Pudding
MONDAY	Corned Beef Hash & Eggs Toast	Minestrone Soup	Ham & Asparagus Strata Peaches
TUESDAY	Oatmeal	Peanut Butter Surprise Sandwich	Rigatoni with Mushroom Sauce Cherry Cobbler
WEDNESDAY	Cheese Omelets Hash Browns Toast	Tuna Salad Wrap	Red Chili with Beef Chunks Corn Bread
THURSDAY	French Toast	Ham Salad Sandwich with Sprouts	Greek Chicken & Lemon Soup with Rice Olive Bread
FRIDAY	Cream of Wheat	Pinto Beans, Tortillas & Salsa	Tuna Casserole Peas Applesauce
SATURDAY	Spam & Eggs Hash Browns Toast	Turkey Salad Wrap with Sprouts	Cottage Pie Mashed Potatoes Cookies

Week 4	BREAKFAST	LUNCH	DINNER
SUNDAY	Veggie Omelets Hash Browns Toast	Tuna Salad Sandwich with Sprouts	Turkey & Asparagus Tetrazzini Pears
MONDAY	Biscuits & Gravy	Macaroni & Cheese	Anasazi Stew Navajo Fry Bread
TUESDAY	Pancakes	Mushroom Barley Soup	Pasta Primavera Apple Crisp
WEDNESDAY	Egg Sandwich	Chicken Salad Sandwich with Sprouts	Hearty Beef & Pasta Bread
THURSDAY	Oatmeal	BBQ Beef Sandwich	Arroz con Pollo Refried Beans Tortillas Pineapple
FRIDAY	French Toast	Shrimp Salad Wrap with Sprouts	Linguine with White Clam Sauce Crostini
SATURDAY	Grits	Peanut Butter Surprise Roll Up	Calico Beans with Sausage & Ground Beef Rolls Rice Pudding

Week 5	**BREAKFAST**	**LUNCH**	**DINNER**
SUNDAY	Swedish Pancakes	Ham Salad Sandwich with Sprouts	Chicken & Black Bean Soup Wild Rice Cakes Chocolate Pudding
MONDAY	Corned Beef Hash & Eggs Toast	Tuna Salad Wrap with Sprouts	Pork Enchiladas Spanish Rice Refried Beans
TUESDAY	Oatmeal	15-Bean Soup Hardtack	Pennette Pasta with Artichoke & Sun-Dried Tomatoes Peach Cobbler
WEDNESDAY	Cheese Omelets Hash Browns, Toast	Turkey Salad Sandwich with Sprouts	Beef Stew on Mashed Potatoes Applesauce
THURSDAY	French Toast	Peanut Butter Surprise Sandwich	Chicken Fried Rice Chinese Noodle Soup
FRIDAY	10-Grain Cereal	Bean & Cheese Burrito	Crab Newburg on Toast with Asparagus Plums
SATURDAY	Creamed Chip Beef on Toast	Chili Mac	Beef Borscht Rolls Cookies

Week ___	BREAKFAST	LUNCH	DINNER
SUNDAY			
MONDAY			
TUESDAY			
WEDNESDAY			
THURSDAY			
FRIDAY			
SATURDAY			

COOKING WITH NO ELECTRICITY

We have all experienced power outages. Fortunately most do not last more that a few hours, but in the event of those lasting for days, we can be greatly inconvenienced. What would you do if the power was out for a week or two? It is always a good idea to have alternative cooking methods on hand to allow you to prepare your meals. Every recipe in this book can be prepared with no electricity by using alternative cooking methods.

Many of us have camping stoves, but make sure to have the propane or white gas on hand in order to use them. Any recipe calling for food to be cooked on a stove top in a pot, pan or on a griddle can easily be prepared on a camping stove as long as there is fuel.

Backyard grills are also a great back up, but make sure you always keep extra full propane tanks or bags of charcoal on hand. Recipes cooked on a stove top in a pot, pan or on a griddle can be cooked on the burner of some propane grills or set on the grill over a gas or charcoal fire as long as there is fuel.

Having a set of different sized Dutch ovens will provide a great source for cooking and baking as long as there is charcoal or wood to burn. Camp Dutch ovens are very versatile. Just about any recipe can be cooked in them. Make sure that you use a cast-iron Camp Dutch oven (with three small legs and the top is flat with a small rim) and not just a cast-iron Dutch oven (with no legs and top is curved with no lip). You can use the Camp Dutch oven as a pot, pan, griddle and as an oven to bake in. They are available in sizes from a small 8-inch oven up to a huge 22-inch oven. When baking in a Camp Dutch oven, set the food in either a smaller Dutch oven inside a larger Camp Dutch oven or use a small round baking pan on a trivet to keep the food directly off the bottom so it won't burn. You can even stack the Dutch ovens one on top of the other (largest on bottom to smallest on top) with charcoals or wood coals on top, underneath and in be-tween them for efficiency when cooking two or three different items. When cooking with coals, always put more on the lid than underneath the oven: $\frac{2}{3}$ on top and $\frac{1}{3}$ on the bottom.

Solar ovens are a fantastic alternative source of free energy, especially if you live in an area of the country that has a lot of sunshine. That means no fuel to store! They are not only easy to use, but nothing will burn or dry out like with electric or gas ovens. The most efficient solar ovens have to be purchased because they come with glass lids that lock and thermostats. However, one can be constructed out of a box and aluminum foil for minimum success. The manufactured solar ovens can reach temperatures up to 400 degrees—so baking, broiling or steaming can be done with only a very small adjustment in cooking time between the high sun hours between 10 a.m. to 2 p.m. It is best to use dark pans and covered casseroles because they will absorb more heat. A solar oven can be preheated by placing a large, round black rock inside it for 15 minutes.

It's also wise to back up your modern, fast, easy, convenient kitchen gadgets with the old-fashioned, elbow-greased counterparts just in case you are without electricity for an extended period of time with items like: a hand-cranked grain mill, an egg-beater (or wire whisk), a non-electric can opener, a hand-cranked food processor, an old-fashioned juicer, a camping toaster, etc.

CONVERTING FRESH INGREDIENTS FOR STORAGE

When looking through recipes to convert to food storage meal, be sure that all of the fresh ingredients can be dried or canned. (However, if you are able to hunt, farm or garden, make cheese, or living on the frozen tundra, you will always have a source of fresh food.

Meals that won't work for most of us include items like steaks, burgers, chops, ribs, roasts, fresh cheeses, lettuce, cucumbers, etc. These are meal ingredients that have to be fresh, refrigerated or frozen and can't just be dried or canned for storage on the pantry shelf.

Look for favorite meals that have the fresh ingredients that can be converted to canned meats and vegetables like stews, goulashes, soups, pasta dishes, and so on. Dairy items like eggs, milk, sour cream, parmesan cheese and cheddar cheeses are available in powdered form for food storage. Breads can be made from freshly-milled whole grains. Most vegetables or fruits can be purchased in cans, jars or dried in packages, or they can be dehydrated or canned in jars at home. There are many meats like beef, pork, poultry and fish available at the store in cans, but with a pressure-cooker, they can also be canned in jars at home.

SHOPPING LISTS

How long does it take to acquire a 1 month, 2 month, 6 month or 1 year supply of food? It all depends on the commitment and attitude you have about the importance of storing food. If you don't already have food storage, or need to update what you've already got, add food storage items to your regular shopping lists. The sooner you start, the faster you can begin to use, rotate, and save money by eating more frequently and conveniently out of your own kitchen!

There are many ways in which to acquire food storage. First you need to decide on how much food storage you'd like to have in your storage: 1 month, 2 months 6 months, or 1 year. The 5-Week Example Menu (see page 15) is equal to a 1-month supply of food. If you want to store a 2-month supply of meals, double it. If you want to store a 6-month supply of food, multiply it by five. For 1-year supply of meals, multiply it by ten.

Creating food storage and shopping lists is simple. You only need to buy items that are necessary to create meals based on the 5-Week Example Menu or your own personalized 5-week menu. To start, look over each meal in Week 1 of your chosen menu. Make a list of every ingredient needed to create each meal. Follow this process for each week so you have five individual lists for each week and the number of weeks you have chosen. Now you are ready to start shopping! Take your lists to the grocery store and buy a few items or meals every time you go, checking them off your list and making sure to date everything you buy and put in storage. This way you can slowly build your food storage without emptying your pocket. This will also help in the rotation of food items because you'll want to use the items before they expire and your don't want them all to expire at once. Just remember to make a list of the items as you use them so you know what needs to be replenished to maintain the amount of storage you have decided on.

FOOD STORAGE BASICS SHOPPING LIST

The following suggested basic food storage list will feed one adult for one year if nothing else is available.

Meats/Dairy:

16 pounds powdered milk

Grains/Beans:

400 pounds (a combination of) whole wheat, oats, rice, macaroni, spaghetti, flour, etc.*

Miscellaneous:

20 pounds or 2 ½ gallons shortening or oil

60 pounds sugar (white sugar, brown sugar, molasses, honey, jams, syrup, etc.)*

8 pounds salt (stored in its original container)

14 gallons water (minimum 2-week supply stored at all times)

*The amount of each item purchased is the buyer's preference. Buy more of what you know you and your family will eat and less of other items.

WHERE DO YOU PUT IT ALL?

Long-term storage items like cases of whole wheat, sugar, salt and dry beans that have been dry packed in #10 cans (which hold approximately 12 cups of food) or 5-gallon buckets can be hidden away in closets, under beds, as a base for a bed, made into tables under tablecloths, hidden behind furniture,etc. All other storage food should always be conveniently accessible on pantry shelves for easy use and rotation.

Your food storage should be located in or around your kitchen. Clean out your kitchen cabinets of seldom-used items such as small appliances, pots and pans, or baking dishes. Store those things in a closet, a large cabinet in the garage, or in the basement or utility room. These items are not affected by extreme hot or cold temperatures like food storage is. Along with the kitchen pantry, use the kitchen cabinets to store food so it is always convenient.

THE PERPETUAL STORAGE CALENDAR

By developing the example 5-Week Storage Menu in a calendar format, the inventory of meals can be easily managed. Make several copies of your five week menu and make each sheet a different month. Write each month's dates over the daily meals (some month's dates will overlap onto different sheets). At the end of each current week, simply highlight the storage meals you didn't use on the week following the end of your acquired storage time frame. Then replace the meals or items that were consumed by adding them to your shopping list to complete this new week. Do the same thing every week and you will always maintain the amount of food storage you have chosen. After you amass your entire storage time frame and fill your shelves with the items, you will become familiar at a glance with the number of items required (you can even mark the quantity on the shelf). If you have chosen a six-month storage plan using the 5-Week Example Menu, you will need to maintain many of the meal's items in multiples of 5. For a one-year plan, multiples of 10 are required.

If you choose to develop your storage plan by using only one, two, three or four weeks of different meals, you can still use the blank 5-Week Storage Menu by simply repeating the weeks to complete the page.

Breakfast

Biscuits & Gravy

Cheese Omelets

Mushroom Omelets

Salsa Omelets

Vegetable Omelets

Corned Beef Hash & Eggs

Creamed Chipped Beef on Toast

Cream of Wheat

Egg Sandwich

French Toast

Grits

Oatmeal

10-Grain Cereal

Pancakes

Swedish Pancakes

Spam & Eggs

BISCUITS & GRAVY

> 2 cups whole wheat flour
> 2 tablespoons baking powder
> 1/4 cup dry milk
> 1 teaspoon salt
> 1/3 cup butter-flavored shortening
> 3/4 cup water
> 2 cans (14.5 ounces each) sausage gravy

Preheat oven to 450 degrees. In a bowl combine flour, baking powder, dry milk and salt. Cut in shortening to resemble coarse meal. Add water and stir until dry ingredients are moistened. Gather dough into a ball and gently knead 5 to 10 times. Transfer to a lightly floured surface and roll out dough to 1/2 inch thick. Cut into 2 1/2-inch rounds with a biscuit cutter or floured drinking glass. Bake on an ungreased baking sheet for 10–12minutes.

Heat the sausage gravy in a pot on range top and pour over biscuits.

Makes 4–6 servings and approximately 12 biscuits.

CHEESE OMELETS

   16 tablespoons dry egg mix (4 tablespoons per omelet)
   16 tablespoons water (4 tablespoons per omelet)
    4 tablespoons butter-flavored shortening or oil
    1 jar/bar (8 ounces) Cheese Whiz or Velveeta
       Salt & pepper

   Mix 4 tablespoons dry egg mix and 4 tablespoons water individually for each omelet.Put1tablespoon shortening or oil in a hot pan and add egg mixture, swirling around in the pan. Cook until set and then flip over carefully. Place one-fourth of the cheese over top and fold in half. Remove omelet from pan onto a plate. Salt and pepper to taste. Serve with hash brown potatoes (see recipe page 114) or toast on the side. Makes 4 servings.

MUSHROOM OMELETS

16 tablespoons dry egg mix (4 tablespoons per omelet)
16 tablespoons water (4 tablespoons per omelet)
 4 tablespoons butter-flavored shortening or oil
 2 cans (4 ounces) mushrooms, drained
   Salt & pepper

Mix 4 tablespoons dry egg mix and 4 tablespoons water individually for each omelet. Put 1 tablespoon shortening or oil in a hot pan and add egg mixture, swirling around in the pan. Cook until set, flip over carefully. Sprinkle one-fourth the mushrooms on top and fold in half. Remove omelet from pan onto a plate. Salt and pepper to taste. Serve with hash brown potatoes (see recipe page 114) or toast on the side. Makes 4 servings.

SALSA OMELETS

16 tablespoons dry egg mix (4 tablespoons per omelet)
16 tablespoons water (4 tablespoons per omelet)
 4 tablespoons butter-flavored shortening or oil
 1 cup salsa (see recipe page 117)
   Salt & pepper

Whisk 4 tablespoons egg mix and 4 tablespoons water individually for each omelet. Put 1 tablespoon shortening or oil in a hot pan and add egg mixture, swirling around in the pan. Cook until set, then flip over carefully. Spread one-fourth the salsa over each omelet and fold in half. Remove omelet from pan onto a plate. Salt & pepper to taste. Serve with hash brown potatoes (see recipe page 114) or toast on the side. Makes 4 servings.

VEGETABLE OMELETS

¼ cup dry onions
¼ cup dry green peppers
1 cup water
16 tablespoons dry egg mix (4 tablespoons per omelet)
16 tablespoons water (4 tablespoons per omelet)
5 tablespoons butter-flavored shortening or oil
1 can (4 ounces) mushrooms, drained
Salt & pepper

Rehydrate the onions and green peppers in 1 cup water for 15 minutes. Drain.

Mix 4 tablespoons dry egg mix and 4 tablespoons water individually for each omelet. Put 1 tablespoon shortening or oil in a hot pan and saute mushrooms, onions and green peppers for 2 minutes. Move vegetables to a bowl and wipe the pan clean. Put 1 tablespoon shortening or oil in the hot pan and add egg mixture, swirling around in the pan. Cook until set, flip over carefully. Place one-fourth the mushrooms, onions and green peppers on top and fold in half. Remove omelet from pan onto a plate. Salt and pepper to taste. Serve with hash brown potatoes (see recipe page 114) or toast on the side. Makes 4 servings.

CORNED BEEF HASH & EGGS

  1 **can (15 ounces) corned beef hash**
12 **tablespoons dry egg mix**
12 **tablespoons water**
  2 **tablespoons butter-flavored shortening or oil**
    Salt & pepper

Spread hash in a pan to fry until lightly browned or in an 8 x 8-inch baking dish and bake at 350 degrees for 25 minutes.

Whisk dry egg mix and water in a bowl. Melt shortening in a pan. Pour in egg mixture and stir until scrambled and set. Divide eggs and hash equally on individual plates. Serve with toast on the side. Makes 4 servings.

CREAMED CHIPPED BEEF ON TOAST

> 4 tablespoons butter-flavored shortening or oil
> 1/4 cup whole wheat flour
> 1/4 teaspoon pepper
> 1 cup dry milk
> 1/2 cup warm water
> 1/2 teaspoon Tabasco sauce
> 1 jar (5 ounces) dried beef
> 8 slices whole wheat bread (see recipe page 107)

In a pot over medium heat, melt shortening or oil. Stir in flour to make a roux. Add pepper. In a bowl, whisk dry milk and warm water together until smooth. Gradually stir milk into roux. Add Tabasco and beef. Continue to simmer until thickened.

Toast the bread and place 4 slices on individual plates. Top each piece of toast with creamed chipped beef. Cut the remaining slices of toast on the diagonal and set on the plates. Makes 4 servings.

CREAM OF WHEAT

1 cup Cream of Wheat
4 cups boiling water
1 teaspoon salt
8 tablespoons brown sugar
½ cup raisins
4 tablespoons chopped almonds (optional)
⅓ cup dry milk + 1 cup warm water, blended

Stir Cream of Wheat into boiling, salted water. Reduce heat to medium and cook 5 minutes, stirring constantly. Remove from heat cover and let stand a few minutes. Divide into individual bowls and sprinkle brown sugar, raisins and nuts over top. Equally divide milk and pour that over toppings. Makes 4 servings.

EGG SANDWICH

- 4 tablespoons mayonnaise
- 2 teaspoons Tabasco sauce
- 8 tablespoons dry egg mix
- 8 tablespoons water
- 2 teaspoons butter-flavored shortening or oil
  Salt & pepper
- 4 tablespoons dried cheese sauce mix
- 8 slices whole wheat bread (see recipe page 107)

In a small bowl, mix mayonnaise and Tabasco sauce together. Set aside. In another bowl, whisk egg mix and water together. In a pan, melt shortening or heat oil. Add egg mixture and scramble until set. Salt and pepper to taste.

Toast bread and spread 4 pieces with mayonnaise sauce. Equally divide the scrambled eggs and place on the remaining toast slices. Sprinkle 1 tablespoon dried cheese over eggs. Place the 4 pieces of toast with mayonnaise sauce over top to make a sandwich. Makes 4 servings.

FRENCH TOAST

  3 cups warm water, divided
  1 cup dry milk
  6 tablespoons dry egg mix
  1 tablespoon sugar
  1 teaspoon vanilla
  8 teaspoons butter-flavored shortening or oil
12 slices whole wheat bread (see recipe page 107)
  8 ounces syrup (or also good with jam)

Put 3 cups warm water in a large bowl and add the dry milk, dry egg mix, sugar and vanilla. Whisk until well blended.

Melt 2 teaspoons shortening or heat oil on a pre-heated griddle or pan. Dip bread into the egg mixture, one at a time, and completely coat and then put on the griddle. Cook until lightly browned on one side, then flip to brown other side. Serve at once. Makes 4–6 servings.

GRITS

½ cup water
½ teaspoon salt
1 cup grits
8 tablespoons sugar
1 cup chopped dried apricots

Bring the water to a boil in a pot. Slowly stir in salt and grits. Reduce heat to medium-low. Cover and cook 5–7 minutes until thickened, stirring occasionally. Remove from heat. Sprinkle sugar and apricots over top. Makes 4 servings.

OATMEAL

2 cups regular rolled oats
$\frac{1}{2}$ teaspoon salt
3 $\frac{1}{2}$ cups boiling water
8 tablespoons brown sugar
$\frac{1}{2}$ cup raisins
4 tablespoons chopped hazelnuts
$\frac{1}{3}$ cup dry milk + 1 cup warm water, blended

Stir oats into rapidly boiling salted water. Reduce heat to medium and cook 5 minutes, stirring constantly. Cover and let stand until desired thickness. Add favorite toppings like brown sugar, raisins, chopped nuts and milk. Makes 4 servings.

10-GRAIN CEREAL

> 2 cups 10-grain cereal
> 6 cups boiling water
> $\frac{1}{2}$ teaspoon salt
> $\frac{1}{3}$ cup dry milk + 1 cup warm water, blended
> 8 tablespoons brown sugar
> $\frac{1}{2}$ cup raisins
> 4 tablespoons chopped walnuts or pecans

Stir cereal into rapidly boiling salted water. Reduce heat to medium and cook 10 minutes, stirring constantly. Cover and let stand until desired thickness.

In a bowl, whisk dry milk and warm water together until smooth. Top cereal with brown sugar, raisins, chopped nuts and mixed milk. Makes 4 servings.

PANCAKES

¾ cup whole wheat flour
¾ cup quick oats
¾ cup oat bran
1 tablespoon baking powder
1 teaspoon baking soda
1 teaspoon salt
⅓ cup dry milk
3 tablespoons dry egg mix
½ teaspoon ground cinnamon
½ teaspoon ground nutmeg
½ cup pecans, chopped (optional)
2 cups water
⅓ cup honey
4 tablespoons butter-flavored shortening, melted
½ teaspoon vanilla
Oil spray for griddle
8 ounces syrup

Mix dry ingredients in a large bowl. Whisk together wet ingredients in another bowl. Pour wet ingredients over the dry ingredients, mixing together just until combined. Ladle ¼ cup batter onto the oiled griddle for each pancake. Cook until the pancake is dotted with bubbles. Turn over carefully and cook until the other side is lightly browned. Makes 4–6 servings.

SWEDISH PANCAKES

    3 tablespoons dry egg mix
    3 tablespoons water
    1 cup dry milk
    3 cups warm water
    4 tablespoons melted butter-flavored shortening or oil
    2 tablespoons sugar
 1 ½ teaspoons salt
 1 ½ cups whole wheat flour
    12 teaspoons butter-flavored shortening or oil
    8 ounces syrup (also good with lingonberries or jam)

Put water and dry egg mix in a bowl and mix with a hand mixer at high speed for 30 seconds. Turn mixer to low speed. Add dry milk, warm water, melted shortening or oil, sugar and salt. Then add the flour, continuing to mix until batter is smooth. Let sit for 5 minutes and mix again. Melt 1 teaspoon shortening or oil in a hot pan. Pour ½ cup batter into the middle, tilting the pan or griddle to form about an 8-inch circle.

Cook until batter sets and edges start to brown a little. Flip carefully and cook other side. Serve at once. Makes 4 servings.

Spam & Eggs

> 1 **can (12 ounces) spam**
> 1 **tablespoon butter-flavored shortening or oil**
> 8 **tablespoons dry egg mix**
> 8 **tablespoons water**
> 2 **tablespoons butter-flavored shortening or oil**
>   **Salt & pepper**

Slice spam into 8 pieces. Melt shortening or heat oil in a pan or on a griddle and fry spam until lightly browned.

Mix dry egg mix and water together in a small bowl. Melt shortening in a pan and add eggs, scrambling until set at a desired consistency. Salt and pepper to taste. Serve with hash brown potatoes (see recipe page 114) or toast on the side. Makes 4 servings.

Lunch

Macaroni & Cheese

Bean & Cheese Burrito

Chili Mac

Sloppy Joes

Pinto Beans

Franks & Beans

15-Bean Soup

Minestrone Soup

Broccoli-Cheese Soup

Mushroom Barley Soup

Split Pea Soup with Spam

Tomato Basil Soup & Cheese Sandwich

BBQ Beef Sandwich

Ham Salad Sandwich

Chicken Salad Sandwich

Peanut Butter Surprise Sandwich/Roll Up

Tuna Salad Sandwich/Wrap

Turkey Salad Sandwich/Wrap

Shrimp Salad Wrap

MACARONI & CHEESE

  6 cups water
  1 teaspoon salt
  2 cups macaroni
  2 tablespoons dry milk + ¼ cup warm water, blended
  1 jar/bar (8 ounces) Cheese Whiz or Velveeta OR
  1 cup dried cheese + ½ cup water

Boil water in a pot and add salt. Add macaroni and cook until almost tender. Drain. Return macaroni to pot and add milk and cheese, stir to mix thoroughly. Add a little milk if too thick. Makes 4 servings.

BEAN & CHEESE BURRITO

　　　　2 cups refried bean flakes
　　　　2 cups boiling water
　　　　1 can (4 ounces) green chiles
　　　　1 teaspoon dried onions
　　　½ teaspoon dried jalapenos
　　　　1 jar/bar (8 ounces) Cheese Whiz or Velveeta OR
　　　　1 cup dried cheese + ½ cup water
　　　　4 whole wheat tortillas (see recipe page 112)

Stir refried bean flakes into boiling water and lower heat. Mix well then add green chiles, onions and jalapenos. Cook over low heat 5 minutes or until thickened. Spread one-fourth of the beans and cheese on each tortilla. Roll up and serve. Makes 4 servings.

CHILI MAC

    1 can (15 ounces) ground beef, drained
    1 tablespoon dried onions
    1 envelope (1.25 ounces) chili seasoning mix
    1 can (15 ounces) stewed tomatoes
    1 can (15 ounces) dark red kidney beans, drained
    1 can (15 ounces) light red kidney beans, drained
    6 cups boiling water
    1 teaspoon salt
    2 cups macaroni

Garnish with:
    ¼ cup dried onion, rehydrated with ½ cup water and drained
    ½ cup dried cheese
    ½ cup dried sour cream, reconstituted with ¼ cup water

In a large pot over high heat, add beef and onions. Add chili seasoning, tomatoes and beans. Turn down heat and simmer for 15 minutes.

In another pot bring salted water to a boil. Add macaroni and cook until almost tender. Drain. Place macaroni into bowls and top with chili. Serve with desired garnishes. Makes 4–6servings.

Sloppy Joes

        2 tablespoons dried onions
        1 can (15 ounces) ground beef, liquid reserved
        2 teaspoons oil
    ½ cup ketchup
        2 tablespoons brown sugar
    ¼ cup water
        2 teaspoons dried mustard
    ½ teaspoon Worcestershire sauce
    ½ teaspoon vinegar
        4 whole wheat rolls (see recipe page 110)
    ½ cup dried cheese + ¼ cup water, blended

Rehydrate the onions in a bowl with the reserved ground beef liquid for 15 minutes.

Heat oil in a pan an add onions. Saute 2 minutes. Add all ingredients except the cheese and bring to a boil. Turn down heat and simmer 15 minutes. Equally divide mixture between rolls. Sprinkle cheese over top. Makes 4 servings.

PINTO BEANS

 2 cups pinto beans
12 cups water
 1 teaspoon salt
 2 tablespoons dried onions
 1 teaspoon dried garlic
 8 cubes beef bouillon
 ½ teaspoon dried red pepper flakes
 ¼ teaspoon cumin
 ½ teaspoon turmeric
 8 whole wheat tortillas (see recipe page 112)
   Salsa (see recipe page 117)

Wash and discard unwanted beans. Put beans into a pot and cover with water on high heat. Add salt, onions, garlic, bouillon, red pepper flakes, cumin and turmeric. Bring to a boil, stirring occasionally for 30 minutes. Turn down heat, cover and simmer approximately 3 hours, or until the beans are tender. Add more water during cooking if necessary. Serve with tortillas and salsa. Makes 4–6 servings.

FRANKS & BEANS

    1 tablespoon shortening
    2 tablespoons dried onions, reconstituted with ¼ cup water
    1 can (28 ounces each) baked beans
    1 tablespoon ketchup
    2 teaspoons brown sugar
    2 cans (5 ounces each) Vienna sausage
    4 slices whole wheat bread (see recipe page 107)
       Danish applesauce (see recipe page 113)

Melt shortening in a pot. Add onions and sauté 1 minute on high heat. Lower heat to medium and add the baked beans, ketchup and brown sugar. Simmer 15 minutes. Add the Vienna Sausage, being careful not to break apart. Cook 5 more minutes. Makes 4 servings.

15-BEAN SOUP

10 ounces (½ package) 15-bean soup mix
9 cups water, divided
¼ cup dried onions
1 can (15 ounces) stewed tomatoes
½ teaspoon red pepper flakes
2 tablespoons lemon juice OR 1 tablespoon dried lemon
½ teaspoon dried garlic
2 cubes vegetable bouillon
Hardtack (see recipe page 113)

Wash and soak beans overnight in 4 cups water. In the morning drain the beans. In a large pot over high heat, add remaining 5 cups water and beans. Bring to a boil. Turn heat down to medium-low and simmer uncovered until the beans are tender, about 1–2 hours. Add onions, tomatoes, red pepper flakes, lemon juice, garlic and bouillon. Simmer 30 minutes more. Correct seasoning. Serve with hardtack (see recipe page 113) or crackers. Makes 4–6 servings.

MINESTRONE SOUP

¼ cup dried onions
¼ cup dried carrots
¼ cup dried celery
2 cups water
1 tablespoon olive oil
1 teaspoon dried garlic
1 can (15 ounces) potatoes, chopped
¼ cup dried zucchini
1 cup sun-dried tomatoes
1 can (15 ounces) cannelloni
½ cups mall shell macaroni
5 cups water
4 cubes beef bouillon
2 teaspoons dried basil
2 teaspoons dried oregano
   Salt & pepper

Rehydrate onions, carrots and celery in 2 cups water for 15 minutes. Drain.

In a large pot over high heat, sauté the onions, carrots, celery and garlic for 2 minutes. Add all other ingredients and bring to a boil. Turn down heat to medium-low and simmer an hour. Correct seasoning. Makes 4–6 servings.

BROCCOLI-CHEESE SOUP

6 to 8 **cups water**
    2 **cups instant potatoes**
    2 **tablespoons dried onions**
    2 **cubes chicken bouillon**
    1 **teaspoon dried parsley**
    1 **jar/bar (8 ounces) Cheese Whiz or Velveeta OR**
    1 **cup dried cheese + $\frac{1}{2}$ cup water**
    1 **cup dried broccoli, reconstituted with 1 cup water**
      Salt and Pepper to taste
      Broccoli sprouts for garnish (see Sprouting section page 132)

In a large pot, heat water until hot and then add potatoes, stirring briskly. Over medium heat add the onions, chicken bouillon, parsley and cheese, mixing well. Add the broccoli with the water and stir in. Turn heat down to low and simmer for 20 minutes. Correct consistency with more water and seasonings if necessary. Sprinkle sprouts on top. Makes 4–6servings.

Mushroom Barley Soup

      ¾ cup dried onions
      ½ cup dried carrots
       3 cups water
       2 cans (4 ounces each) mushrooms, with liquid
  4 to 6 cups water
       8 cubes beef bouillon
       2 tablespoons dried parsley
      ½ cup barley
      ¼ teaspoon black pepper

Rehydrate onions and carrots in 3 cups water for 15 minutes. Drain.
Place the onions and carrots and remaining ingredients in a pot over
high heat. Bring to a boil. Lower heat to medium. Partially cover. Simmer
for 40 minutes or until the barley is tender. Correct seasoning. Makes
4–6servings.

SPLIT PEA SOUP WITH SPAM

      2 cups dried split peas
      ⅓ cup dried carrots
      ⅓ cup dried   celery
      ⅓ cup dried onions
      2 cups water
      8 cups cold water
      1 teaspoon dried garlic
      2 bay leaves
      1 teaspoon thyme
        Salt & pepper
      1 can (12 ounces) Spam

Wash peas. Rehydrate carrots, celery and onions in 2 cups water. Drain. In a large pot bring peas and 8 cups water to a boil. Reduce heat and simmer for 1 hour. Add vegetables and spices and continue to simmer another hour, or until peas are tender.

Cut Spam into bite size pieces and fry in a pan until lightly browned. Add to soup. Makes 4–6 servings.

TOMATO BASIL SOUP & CHEESE SANDWICH

8 teaspoons butter-flavored shortening
8 slices whole wheat bread
1 jar/bar (8 ounces) Cheese Whiz or Velveeta
2 cans(10 ¾ ounces each) tomato soup, condensed
2 cups water
1 teaspoon dried basil
½ teaspoon dried garlic

Spread the shortening on each slice of bread. Place or spread one-fourth of the cheese on the unbuttered side of 4 slices of bread. Preheat pan or griddle and place the bread shortening side down. Top with the remaining 4 slices of bread, shortening side up. Grill until golden brown. Flip over and brown the other side.

In a pot, mix soup and water together until smooth. Add basil and garlic. Cook until heated through, stirring occasionally. Divide into 4 bowls and serve with the grilled cheese sandwiches. Makes 4 servings.

BBQ Beef Sandwich

2 tablespoons dry onions
1 can (15 ounces) beef chunks, reserve liquid
2 teaspoons oil
½ cup ketchup
2 tablespoons brown sugar
¼ cup water
2 teaspoons dried mustard
½ teaspoon Worcestershire sauce
½ teaspoon vinegar
4 whole wheat rolls (see recipe page 110)

Rehydrate the onions in a bowl with the reserved beef liquid for 15 minutes.

Heat oil in a pan and saute onions 2 minutes. Add all ingredients except the beef. Bring to a boil. Turn down heat and simmer 15 minutes. Shred the beef chunks and add to the sauce. Cook 5 minutes more. Serve on whole wheat rolls. Makes 4servings.

Ham Salad Sandwich

    1 **can (16 ounces) ham**
    1 **jar (8 ounces) mayonnaise**
  ¼ **cup sweet pickle relish**
    1 **tablespoon dried onions**
    2 **cups sprouts such as alfalfa, salad mix, broccoli, etc.**
     (see Sprouting section page 132)
    8 **slices whole wheat bread (see recipe page 107)**

Drain ham and place in a bowl. With a fork, break apart the ham into very small pieces. Add ½ cup mayonnaise, relish and onions and mix well.

Spread one-fourth of the mixture on a piece of bread, cover with sprouts and top with another piece of bread that has been spread with more mayonnaise. Makes 4 servings.

Chicken Salad Sandwich

> 1 can (15 ounces) chicken chunks
> 1 jar (8 ounces) mayonnaise
> 2 tablespoons dried celery
> 1 teaspoon dried onions
> 2 cups sprouts
> 8 slices whole wheat bread (see recipe page 107)

Drain chicken chunks. Combine chicken, half the mayonnaise, celery and onions in a bowl and mix well. Spread one-fourth of the mixture on one slice of bread and top with ½ cup sprouts. Spread some of the remaining mayonnaise on the other slice and place on top. Makes 4 servings.

PEANUT BUTTER SURPRISE
SANDWICH/ROLL UP

    8 ounces peanut butter
 4 to 8 tablespoons honey
    1 cup crushed dried banana chips OR 1 cup rehydrated apple
      slices
    1 teaspoon cinnamon
    8 slices whole wheat bread (see recipe page 107) OR
    4 whole wheat tortillas (see recipe page 112

For the sandwich, equally spread the peanut butter on 4 slices of bread. Drizzle the desired amount of honey over peanut butter. Sprinkle one-fourth the banana chips or apple slices over top. Put remaining bread slices over top. Makes 4 servings.

For the roll ups, equally spread the peanut butter on the tortillas. Drizzle the desired amount of honey over peanut butter. Sprinkle one- fourth the banana chips or apple slices over top. Roll up and serve. Makes 4 servings.

TUNA SALAD SANDWICH/WRAP

>   2 cans (6 ounces each) solid white tuna, drained
>   1 can (6 ounces) chunk light tuna, drained
>   1 jar (8 ounces) mayonnaise
>   ¼ cup sweet pickle relish
>   1 tablespoon dried onions
>   2 cups sprouts
>   8 slices whole wheat bread (see recipe page 107) OR
>   4 whole wheat tortillas (see recipe page 112)

For sandwiches, combine tuna, half the mayonnaise, relish and onions in a bowl and mix well. Spread one-fourth of the mixture on one slice of bread and top with ½ cup sprouts. Spread some mayonnaise on the other piece of bread and place on top. Makes 4servings.

For the wraps, spread some mayonnaise on a tortilla and cover with one-fourth of the tuna mixture. Top with ½ cup sprouts, roll up and serve. Makes 4 servings.

TURKEY SALAD SANDWICH/WRAP

1 can (15 ounces) turkey chunks, drained
1 jar (8 ounces)mayonnaise
2 tablespoons dried celery
1 teaspoon dried   onions
2 cups sprouts
8 slices whole wheat bread (see recipe page 107) OR
4 whole wheat tortillas (see recipe page 112)

For sandwiches, combine turkey, half the mayonnaise, celery and onions in a bowl and mix well. Spread one-fourth of the turkey mixture on one slice of bread and cover with ½ cup of sprouts. Spread some mayonnaise on the other slice and place on top. Makes 4 sandwiches.

For the wraps, spread some mayonnaise on the tortilla. Cover with one-fourth of the turkey mixture. Top with ½ cup sprouts, roll up and serve. Makes 4 servings.

SHRIMP SALAD WRAP

   3 cans (6 ounces each) shrimp, drained
   1 tablespoon dried onions
   2 tablespoons dried celery
   1 jar (8 ounces) mayonnaise
   1 teaspoon lemon juice
   1 tablespoon Old Bay seasoning
   1 teaspoon dried dillweed
   4 whole wheat tortillas (see recipe page 112)
   2 cups sprouts

Drain shrimp. Combine shrimp, onions, celery, half the mayonnaise, lemon juice, Old Bay seasoning and dill weed. Mix well. Spread the tortilla with some mayonnaise. Cover with one-fourth of the shrimp salad and top with ½ cup sprouts. Roll up and serve. Makes 4 servings.

Dinner

Anasazi Stew

Beef Stew

Chicken & Dumplings

Cottage Pie

Irish Stew

Beef Borscht

Chicken & Black Bean Soup

Clam Chowder

Greek Chicken Soup

Calico Beans

Red Beans & Rice

Red Chili

White Chili with Chicken

Arroz con Pollo

Chicken Fried Rice

Beef Stroganoff

Chicken Couscous

Fried Ham Dinner

Crab Newburg

Egg Foo Yung

Fettuccini with Capers, Olives, & Tomatoes

Hearty Beef & Pasta

Linguine with White Clam Sauce

Pasta Primavera

Turkey & Asparagus Tettrazini

Spaghetti with Meat Sauce

Pennette Pasta with Artichokes

Rigatoni with Mushroom Sauce

Ham & Asparagus Strata

Green Chile & Chicken Enchiladas

Pork Enchiladas

Smoked Salmon Cakes

Tacos

Tuna Casserole

Turkey & Trimmings

ANASAZI STEW

½ cup dried onions
1 cup dried zucchini
1 cup dried patty pan squash
3 cups water
¼ cup olive oil
4 tablespoons whole wheat flour
1 cup water
1 teaspoon salt
1 teaspoon black pepper
2 cubes beef bouillon
1 can (15 ounces) stewed tomatoes
2 cans (4 ounces each) diced green chiles
1 can (15 ounces) whole kernel corn
1 can (15 ounces) green beans
2 cans (15 ounces each) pork chunks
   Navajo Fry Bread (see recipe page 108)

Rehydrate onions, zucchini and squash in 3 cups water for 15 minutes.
Drain.

In a large pot, heat oil on high. Add flour to make a roux. Stir in water.
Add salt, pepper, bouillon, tomatoes, green chiles, corn, green beans and
pork with the liquid. Bring to a boil and stir until thickened. Add onions,
zucchini and squash. Turn down heat to medium-low and simmer for 30
minutes. Serve with Navajo Fry Bread. Makes 4–6 servings.

BEEF STEW

1 cup dried onions
1 cup dried carrots
3 cups water
2 tablespoons olive oil
½ cup whole wheat flour
3 cups water
1 can (15 ounces) green beans with liquid
1 can (15 ounces) whole kernel corn with liquid
8 to 10 cubes beef bouillon
1 tablespoon dried garlic
1 tablespoon Worcestershire sauce
1 teaspoon Kitchen Bouquet
Salt &pepper
2 cans (15 ounces each) beef chunks, with liquid
Mashed Potatoes (see recipe page 114)

Rehydrate onions and carrots in 3 cups water for 15 minutes. Drain.
In a large pot on high heat, add oil, onions and carrots. Sauté for
1 minute. Sprinkle flour in and lightly brown. Add 3 cups water and stir
until thickened. Add green beans, corn, bouillon, garlic, Worcestershire
sauce, Kitchen Bouquet, and salt and pepper to taste. Turn down heat to
medium-low. Add beef and juice, being careful not to shred the chunks.
Cover. Simmer 30 minutes. Serve stew on top of mashed potatoes heaped
on each plate. Makes 4–6 servings.

CHICKEN & DUMPLINGS

1 cup dried onions
1 cup dried carrots
1 cup dried celery
3 cups water
¼ cup olive oil
1 cup whole wheat flour
10 cups water
14 cubes chicken bouillon
2 bay leaves
1 teaspoon black pepper
1 teaspoon dried thyme
1 teaspoon dried sage
2 tablespoons lemon juice (optional)
2 cans (15 ounces each) chicken chunks, with liquid
Whole Wheat Dumplings (see recipe on next page)
2 tablespoons dried parsley

Rehydrate dried onions, carrots and celery in 3 cups water for 15 minutes. Drain.

Put olive oil in a large pot on high heat, add the vegetables and sauté for 2 minutes. Add the flour and stir well, coating the vegetables. Stir in 10 cups water. Add the bouillon, spices and lemon juice, if using. Bring to a boil and stir until thickened. Add chicken chunks with liquid being careful not to shred the chicken. Drop dumplings onto the boiling stew. Reduce heat and cook, uncovered, 10 minutes. Cover and cook 10minutes more. Sprinkle parsley over top and serve. Makes 4–6 servings.

WHOLE WHEAT DUMPLINGS

    2 cups whole wheat flour
    2 tablespoons baking powder
⅓ cup dry milk
    1 teaspoon salt
    3 tablespoons butter-flavored shortening, melted
    1 cup warm water

  Mix flour, baking powder ,dry milk and salt together in a bowl. Add melted shortening and water. Stir until a soft dough forms. Drop by spoonfuls onto the boiling stew. Reduce heat and cook, uncovered, 10 minutes. Cover and cook 10 minutes more.

COTTAGE PIE

3 tablespoons dried onions
2 tablespoons dried carrots
2 tablespoons dried celery
1 cup water
3 tablespoons olive oil
2 cans (15 ounces each) ground beef, with liquid
½ cup water
1 tablespoon whole wheat flour
4 cubes beef bouillon
1 teaspoon dried thyme
1 teaspoon dried rosemary Pinch of groundnutmeg
Salt &pepper
Mashed Potatoes (see recipe page 114)

In a small bowl, rehydrate onions, carrots and celery in 1 cup water for 15 minutes then drain well.

Preheat oven to 400 degrees. Heat oil in a pan over medium heat and add vegetables, sauté 2 minutes. In a measuring cup add the liquid from the beef to the ½ cup water. Set aside. Add ground beef to the vegetables, constantly stirring to brown evenly. Stir in the flour, mixing well. Add water and liquid from ground beef, bouillon, thyme, rosemary, nutmeg, salt and pepper. Reduce heat to low and simmer 5 minutes until thickened. Transfer to a 9 x 9 inch baking dish and spread mashed potatoes, making peaks, over the top. Bake 30 minutes or until the potatoes start to brown on top. Makes 4–6 servings.

IRISH STEW

              1 cup dried onions
              1 cup dried carrots
              3 cups water
              2 tablespoons oliveoil
              3 bay leaves
            ½ cup whole wheat flour
              3 cups water
     8 to 10 cubes beef bouillon
              1 teaspoon Kitchen Bouquet
              2 teaspoons dried parsley
                Salt &pepper
              2 cans (15 ounces each) beef chunks, with liquid
                Colcannon (see recipe page 106)

Rehydrate onions and carrots in water for 15 minutes. Drain. In a large pot over high heat, add oil. Add bay leaves and let crackle 30 seconds. Remove. Add onions and carrots. Sprinkle flour over vegetables and lightly brown. Add water and stir until thickened. Add bouillon, Kitchen Bouquet, parsley, salt and pepper to taste. Lower heat to medium-low. Add beef, being careful not to shred the chunks. Cover. Simmer 30 minutes. Serve with Colcannon on the side. Makes 4–6 servings.

BEEF BORSCHT

1/2 cup dried onions
1/4 cup dried celery
1/2 cup dried carrots
3 cups dried cabbage
6 cups water
2 tablespoons olive oil
2 cans (15 ounces) sliced beets, with liquid
1 can (15 ounces) stewed tomatoes
1/4 cup vinegar
1 tablespoon dill weed
1 bay leaf
1 teaspoon dried parsley
1 teaspoon black pepper
4 cups water
8 to 10 cubes beef bouillon
1 can (15 ounces) beef chunks, with liquid
1 cup dried sourcream + 1/2 cup water
1 tablespoon dill weed
8 whole wheat rolls (see recipe page 110

Rehydrate onions, celery, carrots and cabbage in 6 cups water for 15 minutes. Drain.

In a large pot over high heat, add oil. Add onions, celery, carrots and cabbage and sauté until lightly browned. Add beets, tomatoes, vinegar, dillweed, bayleaf, parsley, pepper, water, bouillon and beef chunks with liquid. Lower heat to medium-low, cover and simmer 30 minutes. Correct seasonings. In a small bowl, whisk dry sour cream and water together until smooth. Serve in bowls with a dollop of sour cream and dill weed sprinkled on top and rolls on the side. Makes 4–6 servings.

CHICKEN & BLACK BEAN SOUP

¼ cup dried onions
¼ cup dried carrots
1 cup water
2 tablespoons olive oil
2 teaspoons dried garlic
2 dried ancho chiles (poblano) stemmed, seeded and chopped
4 cups water
8 cubes chicken bouillon
2 cups dry black beans
1 teaspoon cumin seeds, toasted and ground
½ cup dried cilantro flakes
2 cans (15 ounces each) chicken chunks, with liquid
2 teaspoons vinegar
Salt & pepper
½ cup dry sour cream + ½ cup water
Salsa (see recipe page 117)

Rehydrate onions and carrots in 1 cup water for 15 minutes. Drain.
In a large pot over high heat, add oil. Add onions, carrots, garlic and chiles. Stir and mix constantly until cooked through. Add 4 cups water, bouillon, black beans and cumin. Turn down heat to medium-low and simmer uncovered for 1 hour or until beans are soft. Add cilantro. (To make this a creamy soup, puree it in a blender then return it to the pot.) Add chicken and heat through. Add vinegar and salt and pepper to taste. In a small bowl, mix dry sour cream and water until smooth. Garnish with sour cream and salsa. Makes 4–6 servings.

CLAM CHOWDER

 4 tablespoons olive oil
 ½ cup whole wheat flour
 8 to 10 cups water
 12 cubes chicken bouillon
 ½ cup dried celery
 ½ cup dried onion
 1 can (15 ounces) potatoes, chopped
 3 cans (6.5 ounces each) clams, with liquid
 1 teaspoon thyme
 2 tablespoons dried green pepper
 1 can (15 ounces) stewed tomatoes, drained and rinsed
 Hardtack (see recipe page 113)

In a large pot on medium-high heat, add oil. Add flour and make a roux. Add water, bouillon, celery, onion, potatoes, clams, thyme, green pepper, and pulp only from can of stewed tomatoes. Simmer 30 minutes on medium heat. Serves 4. Serve with Hardtack on the side. Makes 4–6 servings.

GREEK CHICKEN SOUP

    4 tablespoons olive oil
    ½ cup whole wheat flour
8 to 10 cups water
   12 cubes chicken bouillon
    2 cans (15 ounces) chicken chunks, with liquid
    ½ cup lemon juice OR 2 tablespoons dried lemon
    ¾ cup rice
      Olive Bread (see recipe page 109)

In a large pot on medium-high heat, add oil. Add flour and make a roux. Add water, bouillon, chicken chunks, lemon juice and rice. Turn heat to medium-low and simmer 30 minutes. Correct seasonings. Serve with Olive Bread on the side. Makes 4–6 servings.

CALICO BEANS

½ cup dried onions
1 cup water
1 can (15 ounces) ground beef, drained
1 can (15 ounces) sausage, drained
1 jar (3 ounces) real bacon bits
1 can (15 ounces) baked beans, with liquid
1 can (15 ounces) red kidney beans, with liquid
1 can (15 ounces) lima beans, drained
1 can (15 ounces) butter beans, drained
½ cup ketchup
2 tablespoons vinegar
¼ cup brown sugar
2 tablespoons sugar
2 teaspoons dry mustard powder
1 teaspoon yellow mustard
8 whole wheat rolls (see recipe page 110)

Rehydrate onions in 1 cup water for 15 minutes. Drain.

Pour all of the ingredients into a 9 x 13-inch baking dish. Mix well. Bake, uncovered, at 350 degrees for 1 hour. Serve with rolls on the side. Makes 4–6 servings.

Red Beans & Rice

  1 bag (16 ounces) small red beans
10 cups water
  ½ cup dried onions
  ½ cup dried celery
  ¼ cup dried green pepper
  1 tablespoon dried parsley
  2 bay leaves
  1 tablespoon dried minced garlic
  2 tablespoons olive oil
  1 teaspoon cracked pepper
  1 teaspoon salt
  1 tablespoon Worcestershire sauce
  1 tablespoon Tabasco sauce (optional)
  4 cups cooked rice (see recipe page 116)

Soak the beans in 10 cups water overnight or first thing in the morning. Three hours before dinner, drain the beans and place them back into the pot. Add the onions, celery, green pepper, parsley, bay leaves, garlic and enough water to cover the contents. Bring to a boil then turn down to medium heat and simmer, uncovered for 2 hours. Add more water if necessary. Then, add the olive oil, pepper, salt, Worcestershire sauce and Tabasco sauce, if using. Turn the heat down to low, cover the pot, and continue to cook for 1 more hour. Correct the seasonings. Serve over rice. Makes 4–6 servings.

RED CHILI

2 cans (15 ounces each) beef chunks, drained
2 tablespoons dried onions
2 envelopes (1.25 ounces) chili seasoning mix
1 can (15 ounces) stewed tomatoes
1 can (15 ounces) tomato sauce
1 can (15 ounces) dark red kidney beans, drained
1 can (15 ounces) light red kidney beans, drained
¼ cup dried onion, reconstituted in ½ cup water, then drained
½ cup dried sour cream, reconstituted with ¼ cup water
Corn Bread (see recipe page 106)

Add first seven ingredients to a large pot and bring to a boil. Turn down heat and simmer for 15 minutes. Serve with onions and sour cream on top and corn bread on the side. Makes 4–6 servings.

WHITE CHILI WITH CHICKEN

    3 tablespoons dried onions + ½ cup water
    1 tablespoon olive oil
    1 tablespoon dried garlic
    1 teaspoon cumin
    1 teaspoon tumeric
    2 cans (15 ounces each) chicken chunks, with liquid
    1 can (15 ounces) butter beans, drained
    1 can (15 ounces) hominy (white corn), drained
    1 can (15 ounces) Great Northern beans, drained
    1 can (15 ounces) pinto beans, drained
    1 can (28 ounces) green chile enchilada sauce
    3 cans (4 ounces each) diced green chiles
    8 whole wheat tortillas (see recipe page 112)

Soak dried onions in water for 10 minutes. Drain. Heat olive oil in a pot. Add onions, garlic, cumin and tumeric. Cook 2 minutes on high heat. Lower heat and add chicken, beans and corn. Add enchilada sauce and green chiles. Cook on low heat for 30 minutes. Serve with tortillas and pineapple rings on the side. Make 4–6 servings.

Arroz con Pollo

⅓ cup dried onions
¼ cup dried green peppers
2 cups water
2 tablespoons oil
1 tablespoon garlic
1 cup uncooked rice
½ teaspoon cumin
½ teaspoon tumeric
1 can (15 ounces) diced tomatoes
1 can (4 ounces) diced green chiles
1 can (4 ounces) chopped jalapenos
1 cup water
4 cubes chicken bouillon
2 cans (15 ounces) chicken chunks, with broth
½ cup dried peas + 1 cup water
½ cup green olives with pimientos, sliced
1 tablespoon capers
½ cup dried sour cream + ½ cup water
    Refried Beans (see recipe page 117)
    8 tortillas (see recipe page 111)

Rehydrate onions and green peppers in 2 cups water for 15 minutes. Drain.

In a large pot, heat oil on high and sauté onions, green peppers and garlic until lightly browned. Stir in rice. Add cumin, tumeric, tomatoes, green chiles, jalapenos (or serve on side),water, bouillon and broth from the canned chicken. Bring to a boil. Add the chicken chunks on top and cover. Reduce heat to medium-low and simmer 25 minutes or until rice is tender and liquid is absorbed. Remove from heat.

Rehydrate peas in 1 cup water for 15 minutes. Drain.

Sprinkle peas, olives and capers on top. Cover and let stand for 10 minutes.

In a small bowl, mix dried sour cream with water until smooth and creamy. Serve chicken mixture on warm tortillas with sour cream on top and refried beans on the side. Makes 4–6 servings.

CHICKEN FRIED RICE

¼ cup dried carrots
¼ cup dried green peas
¼ cup dried green onions
1 cup water
2 tablespoons dry egg mix + 2 tablespoonswater
½ cup olive oil
2 cans (15 ounces each) chicken chunks, drained
1 envelope (¾ounce) fried rice seasoning mix
4 cups cold, cooked rice (see recipe page 116)
2 tablespoons soy sauce
½ teaspoon salt
½ teaspoon black pepper
Chinese Noodle Soup (see recipe page 105)

Rehydrate carrots, peas and green onions in 1 cup water for 15 minutes. Drain. Set aside.

Mix dried egg mix and water together. Heat oil in a wok pan and stir fry chicken for 2 minutes, lightly browning. Add the egg mixture and scramble well. Add seasoning mix, rice, soy sauce, salt and pepper constantly stirring until hot and well mixed. Add carrots, peas and onions and continue to stir fry 3 minutes. Serve with Chinese Noodle Soup. Makes 4–6 servings.

BEEF STROGANOFF

      1 cup dried onions + 1 cup water
      ¼ cup olive oil
      ¾ cup whole wheat flour
      1 teaspoon salt
      1 teaspoon pepper
  4 to 6 cups water
      1 tablespoon dried garlic
8 to 10 cubes beef bouillon
      3 cans (4 ounces each) sliced mushrooms, with liquid
      1 tablespoon Worcestershire sauce
      3 tablespoons ketchup
      2 cans (15 ounces each) beef chunks, with liquid
      1 cup dried sour cream + ½ cup water
      6 cups uncooked wide noodles
    10 cups water
      1 teaspoon salt

Rehydrate onions in water for 15 minutes. Drain. Pour olive oil into a large pot on high heat. Add onions and cook 2 minutes. Add flour, salt and pepper and mix well with oil and onions, then pour in water and continue to mix. Add garlic, bouillon, mushrooms with liquid, Worcestershire sauce, ketchup and liquid from beef chunks. Turn heat down to medium and continue to stir and thicken for 30 minutes. Add beef, being careful not to break apart the chunks too much. Mix dried sour cream and water in a small bowl. Stir into the beef stew.

Boil 10 cups salted water in a large pot. Add noodles and cook until tender. Drain well and then serve beef mixture over noodles. Makes 4–6 servings.

CHICKEN COUSCOUS

   1 **tablespoon olive oil**
   1 **teaspoon dried garlic**
   1 **cup sun-dried tomatoes,chopped**
   2 **cans (15 ounces each) chicken chunks, with liquid**
   1 **cup water**
   2 **cubes chicken bouillon**
  ⅓ **cup raisins**
1 ½ **cups couscous**
   2 **tablespoons dried parsley**
   3 **tablespoons dried lime, crushed**
    Salt &pepper

In a pan, heat oil over medium heat. Add garlic and tomatoes. Cook until heated through. Add chicken chunks with broth, water, bouillon and raisins. Bring to a boil. Stir in couscous and cover. Remove from heat and let sit 5 minutes. Uncover. Add parsley, lime and salt & pepper to taste. Toss gently. Makes 4 servings.

FRIED HAM DINNER

    1 can (16 ounces)ham
    2 tablespoons butter-flavored shortening or oil
    1 can (15 ounces) creamed corn
    1 can (15 ounces) whole kernel corn, drained
    1 can (15 ounces) green beans
    1 can (29 ounces) sweet potatoes
    2 tablespoons brown sugar

Slice ham into 8 pieces. Melt shortening or heat oil in a pan and fry ham until lightly browned.

In a pot, mix together creamed corn and whole kernel corn and heat.Heat green beans in another small pot and warm sweet potatoes in a third small pot. Add brown sugar and mash or leave in chunks.

Equally divide the ham, corn, green beans and sweet potatoes on individual plates. Makes 4 servings.

CRAB NEWBURG

    4 tablespoons butter-flavored shortening or oil
    2 tablespoons whole wheat flour
    ¼ teaspoon salt
    ¼ teaspoon nutmeg
    ½ teaspoon paprika
    ¾ cup dry milk + 1 ½ cups warm water, blended
    3 cans (6 ounces each) crab meat, drained
    2 tablespoons dry sherry (optional)
    1 can (15 ounces) asparagus spears
    8 slices whole wheat bread (see recipe page 107)

In a pot over medium heat, melt shortening or heat oil. Stir in flour to make a roux. Add salt, nutmeg and paprika. Gradually stir milk into pot. Add crab meat and sherry. Continue to simmer until thickened, about 10minutes.

In another pot warm asparagus and then drain.

Toast bread and place asparagus on top of toast and pour crab mixture over asparagus. Makes 4 servings.

EGG FOO YUNG

8 tablespoons dried egg mix + 8 tablespoons water
1 can (8 ounces) water chestnuts, drained and chopped
¼ cup dried celery
1 can (15 ounces) bean sprouts, drained (or 2 cups fresh bean sprouts)
8 dried shiitake mushrooms, soaked 2 hours and chopped
¼ cup dried onions
1 teaspoon salt
1 teaspoon black pepper
8 tablespoons olive oil
Chinese Brown Sauce (see recipe page 104)
Pork Fried Rice (see recipe page 115)

In a large bowl, combine dried egg mix and water. Add water chestnuts, celery, bean sprouts, mushrooms, onions, salt and pepper. Stir lightly. For each Egg Foo Yung pour 1 tablespoon oil on a hot griddle and ladle about ½ cup of mixture onto griddle. Cook until lightly browned then turn over carefully and brown on the other side. Place into a baking dish to keep warm until all eight are cooked. Pour Chinese Brown Sauce over them and serve with Pork Fried Rice. Makes 4 servings.

Fettuccini with Capers, Olives, & Tomatoes

  1 tablespoon olive oil
  1 tablespoon minced dried garlic
  2 tablespoons dried onion
  2 cans (14.5 ounces each) stewed tomatoes
  2 tablespoons capers
  1 can (15 ounces) black olives, drained and halved
  1 tablespoon spicy spaghetti or Italian seasoning
  1 teaspoon red pepper flakes 1 teaspoon salt
  1 tablespoon dried oregano
 ½ teaspoon salt
12 cups boiling water
 8 ounces fettuccini
 ½ cup grated Parmesan cheese

Heat oil in a pot. Add garlic and onion and sauté for 1 minute. Lower heat to medium and add tomatoes, capers, olives, seasoning, red pepper flakes, salt and oregano. Simmer for 30 minutes.

In another large pot, boil salted water. Add fettuccini and cook al dente (tender, but firm). Drain. Add fettuccini to the sauce and mix well. Equally divide onto plates and sprinkle with Parmesan cheese. Makes 4 servings.

HEARTY BEEF & PASTA

½ cup dried onions
½ cup dried green pepper
2 cups water
3 teaspoons dried garlic
2 tablespoons olive oil
1 can (15 ounces) beef chunks, with liquid
1 can (15 ounces) ground beef, with liquid
1 jar (24 ounces) spaghetti sauce
1 can (15 ounces) stewed tomatoes
1 can (6 ounces) tomato paste 4 to 6 cups water
8 to 10 cubes beef bouillon
2 tablespoons spicy spaghetti or Italian seasoning
1 teaspoon basil
¼ teaspoon sugar
Salt & pepper
1 teaspoon red pepper flakes
12 ounces pipette pasta (or any variety)
8 slices whole wheat bread (see recipe page 107)

Rehydrate onions and green pepper in 1 cup water for 15 minutes and then drain.

In a large pot on high heat, sauté onions ,green pepper and garlic for 1 minute in oil. Add all of the ingredients including the uncooked pasta. Turn down heat to medium-low and cover. Adjust the consistency with water while it simmers for 30 minutes. Makes 4–6 servings.

LINGUINE WITH WHITE CLAM SAUCE

¼ cup olive oil
2 teaspoons dried garlic
2 tablespoons whole wheat flour
3 cans (6.5 ounces each) chopped clams, with liquid
½ cup dry white wine
1 bay leaf
1 teaspoon oregano
½ teaspoon red pepper flakes
1 tablespoon dried parsley
   Salt & pepper
8 cups water
1 teaspoon salt
1 package (8 ounces) linguine
1 cup Parmesan cheese
   Crostini (see recipe page 108)

In a medium pot over medium heat, add oil and garlic and sauté 1 minute. Stir in flour. Add clam juice, wine, bay leaf, oregano, red pepper flakes, and parsley. Simmer for 10 minutes. Add clams and heat through. Add salt and pepper to taste.

In a large pot, bring salted water to a boil. Add linguine and cook al dente (until almost tender). Drain.

Serve sauce over linguine. Sprinkle with parmesan cheese. Serve crostini on the side. Makes 4 servings.

PASTA PRIMAVERA

½ cup dried onions
1 cup water
½ cup dried broccoli
¼ cup dried carrots
1 cup dried sweet peppers
3 cups water
3 teaspoons dried garlic
2 tablespoons olive oil
1 can (4 ounces) mushrooms, with liquid
2 teaspoons dried basil
1 teaspoon red pepper flakes
¼ cup whole wheat flour
Salt & pepper
¼ cup dry milk
½ cup dry sour cream
1 cup warm water
2 teaspoons dried parsley
8 cups water
1 teaspoon salt
1 package (8 ounces) linguine
1 cup Parmesan cheese

Rehydrate onions in 1 cup water for 15 minutes then drain. Rehydrate broccoli, carrots and peppers in another bowl with 3 cups water for 15 minutes and then drain and set aside.

In a large pot over high heat, sauté onions and garlic in olive oil for 1 minute. Add broccoli, carrots, peppers, mushrooms, basil and red pepper flakes. Turn heat down to medium. Add flour. Add salt and pepper to taste.

In a bowl, mix dry milk, dry sour cream and warm water with a whisk until smooth. Add to the pot to thicken. Correct consistency by adding water to make a creamy sauce.

In another large pot, bring salted water to a boil. Add linguine and cook al dente (until almost tender). Drain.

Pour vegetable mixture over linguine and sprinkle the cheese and parsley on top. Makes 4–6 servings.

Turkey & Asparagus Tettrazini

        4 tablespoons olive oil
        ½ cup whole wheat flour
        1 cup dry milk
     3 ½ cups water
        8 cubes chicken bouillon
        1 teaspoon salt
        1 can (10.75 ounces) cream asparagus soup, condensed
        2 tablespoons dry sherry(optional)
        2 cans (15 ounces each) turkey chunks, with liquid
        1 can (15 ounces) asparagus, with liquid
        8 cups water
        1 teaspoon salt
        1 package (8 ounces) spaghetti
        1 cup Parmesan cheese

Heat oil in a large pot over medium heat. Add flour to make a roux. Mix warm water and dry milk together in a bowl, whisking until smooth and add to roux. Add bouillon, salt, soup, sherry, and liquid from the turkey and asparagus. Turn heat to low and simmer 5 minutes. Put half the sauce into a bowl and add the turkey and asparagus. Leave the other half of the sauce in the pot, turn off heat andcover.

In another large pot bring salted water to a boil and cook the spaghetti al dente (until almost tender). Drain. Add cooked spaghetti to the bowl of turkey mixture. Mix well. Pour into a greased 9 x 13-inch baking dish. Sprinkle the cheese on top. Cover. Place in a preheated 350-degree oven and bake for 30 minutes. Warm the sauce in the pot and pour on top and serve. Makes 4–6 servings.

SPAGHETTI WITH MEAT SAUCE

1 can (15 ounces each) ground beef, drained
1 tablespoon driedonions
2 teaspoons dried garlic
2 jars (24 ounces each) spaghetti sauce
2 tablespoons spicy spaghetti or Italian seasoning
1 can (4 ounces) sliced mushrooms
1 cup Parmesan cheese
8 cups water
1 teaspoon salt
1 package (16 ounces) angel hair pasta
Crostini (see recipe page 108)

Put ground beef in a pot. Add dried onions and garlic and cook over high heat for 2 minutes. Turn down heat and add spaghetti sauce, seasoning and mushrooms. Let simmer for 20 minutes. Serve over pasta andsprinkle with Parmesan cheese.

For pasta, bring a large pot of salted water to a boil. Add pasta and cook al dente, until almost tender, approximately 5 to 7 minutes. Serve with crostini on the side. Makes 4 servings.

PENNETTE PASTA WITH ARTICHOKES

   2 teaspoons dried garlic
   3 tablespoons olive oil
   1 jar (32 ounces) marinated artichokes, with liquid
   1 cup sun-dried tomatoes
   2 tablespoons pepper jardinière
   1 tablespoon dried parsley
   1 teaspoon spicy spaghetti or Italian seasoning
   2 tablespoons Italian bread crumbs
     Salt &pepper
  10 cups water
   1 teaspoon salt
   1 package (16 ounces) pennette pasta
  ½ cup parmesan cheese

   In a medium pot over medium-high heat, sauté garlic in olive oil
1 minute. Add artichokes, tomatoes, jardinière, parsley, Italian seasoning,
bread crumbs and salt & pepper to taste. Simmer 5 minutes.

   In a large pot, bring salted water to a boil. Add pasta and cook al dente
(until almost tender) then drain. Toss pasta with sauce and top with cheese.
Makes 4–6 servings.

Rigatoni with Mushroom Sauce

1 tablespoon olive oil
1 tablespoon butter-flavored shortening
1 tablespoon dried garlic
½ teaspoon red pepper
4 cans (4 ounces each) sliced mushrooms, with liquid
½ cup water
4 cubes chicken bouillon
2 tablespoons parsley
10 cups water
1 teaspoon salt
1 package (16 ounces) rigatoni
½ cup parmesan cheese

In a pan on high, heat oil and butter shortening. Add garlic and red pepper. Cook 30 seconds. Add mushrooms with liquid, water and bouillon. Cook until thickened. Stir in parsley.

Boil salted water in a pot and add rigatoni. Cook al dente (until almost tender). Drain. Pour mushroom sauce over pasta and mix well. Add cheese. Makes 4–6 servings.

HAM & ASPARAGUS STRATA

  1 cup warm water
  8 tablespoons dry egg mix
  ¼ cup dry milk
    Salt & pepper
  1 tablespoon olive oil
12 slices whole wheat bread
  1 can (16 ounces) ham, sliced thin
  2 cans (15 ounces each) asparagus spears
  1 bar (8 ounces) Velveeta, sliced thin

In a bowl, whisk water, dry egg mix, dry milk and salt & pepper until smooth. Spread oil in an 8 x 8-inch baking dish. Line the bottom with 4 slices of bread. Cover with a third of the ham. Line up a third of the asparagus, alternating ends across top. Cover with a third of the cheese. Add two more layers of bread, ham, asparagus and cheese. Pour the egg mixture evenly over the top layer. Cover with plastic wrap and chill overnight. Bake in a preheated 350-degree oven for 35–40 minutes. Let stand 5 minutes before cutting. Makes 4 servings.

Green Chile & Chicken Enchiladas

> 1 tablespoon dried onions + $\frac{1}{2}$ cup water
> 1 can (4 ounces) diced green chiles
> 1 can (14.5 ounces) green chile enchilada sauce
> 1 can (28 ounces) green chile enchilada sauce
> 2 cans (15 ounces each) chicken chunks, drained
> 12 whole wheat tortillas (see recipe page 112)
> 1 jar/bar (8 ounces) Cheese Whiz or Velveeta OR 12 tablespoons dried cheese sauce mix
> 1 can (28 ounces) green chile enchilada sauce
> $\frac{1}{2}$ cup dried cheese sauce mix
> 1 cup dried sour cream + $\frac{1}{2}$ cup water
> $\frac{1}{2}$ cup dried green onions

Rehydrate onions in water for 15 minutes then drain. Place in a large bowl with diced green chiles, green chile sauce, and chicken chunks. Mix well. Spread each tortilla with cheese and one-twelfth of the filling. Roll up burrito style.

Pour half of the 28-ounce can of green chile sauce in the bottom of a 9 x 13-inch baking dish and place rolled up tortillas on top in a single layer. Pour the remaining green chile sauce on top of the tortillas and sprinkle with $\frac{1}{2}$ cup dried cheese. Bake in a preheated 350-degree oven for 30 minutes. Mix dried sour cream with water. Top each serving with sour cream and green onions. Makes 4–6 servings.

PORK ENCHILADAS

½ cup dried onions + 1 cup water
2 cans (28 ounces each) red chili enchilada sauce
2 cans (15 ounces each) pork chunks, drained
12 whole wheat tortillas (see recipe page 112
1 jar/bar (8 ounces) Cheese Whiz orVelveeta OR 12 tablespoons dried cheese sauce mix
½ cup dried cheese sauce mix
Refried Beans (see recipe page 117)
Spanish Rice (see recipe page 116)

Rehydrate onions in water for 15 minutes. Drain. Place in a large bowl with 1 can of enchilada sauce and pork chunks. Mix well. Spread each tortilla with cheese. Roll up burrito style.

Pour the other half of the second can of enchilada sauce in the bottom of a 9 x 13-inch baking dish and place filled tortillas on top in a single layer. Pour the remaining sauce over top of the tortillas and sprinkle with dried cheese. Bake in a preheated 350-degree oven for 30 minutes. Serve with Refried Beans and Spanish Rice on the side. Makes 4–6 servings.

SMOKED SALMON CAKES

¼ cup dried onions
¼ cup dried celery
1 cup water
3 cans (7 ounces each) salmon, drained
1 tablespoon liquid smoke
1 tablespoon lemon juice or 2 teaspoons dried lemon
1 teaspoon dried dillweed
2 teaspoons Worcestershire sauce
5 drops Tabasco sauce
¼ cup oat bran
3 tablespoons dry egg mix + 3 tablespoons water
1 cup olive oil
1 cup dry breadcrumbs
2 cans (15 ounces each) stewed tomatoes

Rehydrate onions and celery in 1 cup water for 15minutes. Drain. Place in a bowl. Add salmon, liquid smoke, lemon juice, dill weed, Worcestershire sauce, Tabasco sauce, oat bran and egg/water mixture and combine well. Chill, covered, 1 hour. Heat oil in a pan ¼ inch deep. Shape salmon mixture into 8 cakes and roll in bread crumbs. Sauté in oil, turning until golden brown on both sides. Drain on paper towels. Warm stewed tomatoes in a pot. Scoop tomatoes onto plates and place salmon cakes over top. Makes 4 servings.

TACOS

¼ cup dried onions
½ cup water
2 cans (15 ounces each) ground beef, with liquid
1 envelope (1.25 ounces) taco seasoning mix
12 taco shells (boxed) or soft corn tortillas
   (see recipe page 111)
1 cup alfalfa sprouts
12 tablespoons dried cheese sauce mix
1 can (15 ounces) diced tomatoes, drained
1 bottle (12 ounces) taco sauce
Refried Beans (see recipe page 117)
Salsa (see recipe page 117)

Rehydrate onions in a small bowl of water for 15 minutes. Drain. Set aside for topping.

In a pan over high heat, add ground beef. Add seasoning mix. Reduce heat to medium. Simmer 5 minutes. Fill taco shells with meat and add sprouts, cheese and tomatoes.

Set tacos on individual plates with Refried Beans and Salsa on the side. Makes 4–6 servings.

TUNA CASSEROLE

4 tablespoons butter-flavored shortening or oil
2 cans (4 ounces each) sliced mushrooms
2 tablespoons dried red or green peppers
2 tablespoons dried onions
¼ cup whole wheat flour
¾ cup dry milk
2 ½ cups water
1 jar/bar (8 ounces) Cheese Whiz or Velveeta OR 1 cup dried cheese sauce mix
2 cans (6 ounces each) solid white tuna, drained
1 can (6 ounces) chunk light tuna, drained
8 cups water
½ teaspoon salt
1 ½ cups wide egg noodles
2 tablespoons dried parsley
Salt & pepper
½ cup dry bread crumbs
2 tablespoons butter shortening, melted

In a pot over medium heat, melt butter shortening until bubbly. Add mushrooms, peppers and onions. Cook 5 minutes. Remove from heat. Stir in flour and dry milk and mix thoroughly. Return to heat. Whisk in water until mixture returns to a boil and thickens. Remove from heat and stir in cheese until melted.

In a large bowl flake apart the tuna, leaving it in small chunks. Pour in the hot cheese sauce. Mix together.

In another pot bring the salted water to a boil. Stir in the egg noodles and cook al dente (until almost tender). Drain. Add the noodles, parsley and salt & pepper to the bowl. Mix together well. Pour the tuna mixture into a greased 9 x 13-inch baking dish. Mix the dry bread crumbs and melted butter together in a dish. Sprinkle over the tuna mixture. Bake in a preheated 375-degree oven for about 30 minutes, until bubbly and browned on top. Makes 4–6 servings.

TURKEY & TRIMMINGS

  ½ cup olive oil
  1 cup whole wheat flour
  3 cans (15 ounces each) turkey chunks
6 to 8 cups water
  8 chicken bouillon cubes
  1 teaspoon Kitchen Bouquet
   Stuffing (use boxed or see recipe page 118)
   Mashed Potatoes (see recipe page 114)
  1 can (15 ounces) green beans, warmed
  1 can (15 ounces) whole cranberry sauce

Make a roux by heating the oil in a large pot and adding the flour, mixing until all of the oil is absorbed. Add the liquid from the cans of turkey and the water. Continue to stir as the mixture thickens. Add bouillon and Kitchen Bouquet, turn the heat down and simmer for 15 to 20 min utes. Correct consistency and seasoning. Add turkey chunks, being careful not to shred them. Simmer 5 more minutes. Serve over mashed potatoes and stuffing. Serve the warmed green beans and chilled cranberry sauce on the side. Makes 4–6 servings.

Sides and Sauces

Chinese Brown Sauce

Chinese Noodle Soup

Colcannon

Corn Bread

Healthy Whole Wheat Bread

Crostini

Navajo Fry Bread

Olive Bread

Whole Wheat Rolls/Bread

Corn Tortillas

Whole Wheat Tortillas

Danish Applesauce

Hardtack

Hash Brown Potatoes

Mashed Potatoes

Pork Fried Rice

Rice

Spanish Rice

Refried Beans

Salsa

Stuffing

Wild Rice Cakes

CHINESE BROWN SAUCE

    2 tablespoons cornstarch
    ½ cup cold water
2 ½ cups water
    4 cubes chicken bouillon
    2 teaspoons soy sauce
    1 teaspoon Kitchen Bouquet
    ½ teaspoon sugar
    ½ teaspoon black pepper

In a small bowl, mix cornstarch with ½cup cold water. Combine all ingredients in a saucepan and bring to a boil. Reduce heat and simmer until thickened, stirring constantly. Makes about 2cups.

CHINESE NOODLE SOUP

12 dried shiitake mushrooms
2 cups water
6 cups hot water
4 ounces angel hair pasta
7 cups water
8 cubes chicken   bouillon
2 cups dried cabbage
½ teaspoon black pepper
1 tablespoon dried green onions
2 tablespoons dried parsley flakes
1 tablespoon dried carrots

In a bowl, soak the mushrooms in 2 cups water for 30 minutes. Drain, rinse,and thinly slice. In a medium pot, bring 6 cups water to a boil and cook pasta al dente (until almost tender). Drain and set aside.

In a large pot over high heat, bring 7 cups of water to a boil. Stir in the bouillon, mushrooms, cabbage, pepper, green onions, parsley and carrots. Lower heat to medium and simmer uncovered for 10 minutes. Divide pasta into four bowls. Spoon out vegetables from broth and place on pasta. Ladle out broth and fill each bowl. Makes 4 servings.

Colcannon

    1 cup dried shredded cabbage
    1 cup water
    2 tablespoons butter-flavored shortening
    1 teaspoon salt
    2 cups Mashed Potatoes (see recipe page 114)

Rehydrate cabbage in 1 cup water for 15 minutes then drain.
In a pot, melt shortening. Add cabbage and salt. Cook until cabbage is hot. Add to potatoes and mix well. Makes 4 servings.

Corn Bread

1 ¼ cups cornmeal
    ¾ cup whole wheat flour
    2 tablespoons sugar
    1 tablespoon baking powder
    1 teaspoon baking soda
    ½ teaspoon salt
    2 tablespoons dry egg mix
    ½ cup dry milk 1 ⅓ cups water
    3 tablespoons melted butter-flavored shortening

In a large bowl, whisk together the dry ingredients. In another bowl, whisk together the wet ingredients. Add the wet ingredients to the dry and stir until just moistened. Pour into a greased 9 x 9-inch baking dish. Tilt dish to spread out evenly. Place on the center rack of a preheated 425-degree oven. Bake for 20 to 25 minutes. Makes 4–6 servings.

HEALTHY WHOLE WHEAT BREAD

3 cups warm water
2 tablespoons or 2 packages active dry yeast
2 tablespoons honey
2 tablespoons olive oil
3 teaspoons salt
1 tablespoon dry egg mix + 1 tablespoon water
3 tablespoons wheat germ
½ cup soy flour
¾ cup dry milk
6 cups whole wheat flour, or more if necessary
2 tablespoons sesame seeds (optional)
3 tablespoons sunflower seeds (optional)

Blend all ingredients in a mixer bowl with a dough hook or work by hand. Add flour to knead and shape up. Place dough in a large greased bowl. Cover and let rise in a warm place until double in size, approximately 40 minutes. Punch down and shape into 3 loaves. Place into greased bread pans and let rise again until doubled. Bake in a 400-degree oven for 15 minutes. Reduce temperature to 350 degrees and continue to bake for 45 minutes or until loaves are a golden brown and sound hollow when tapped. Makes 3 loaves.

CROSTINI

⅓ cup olive oil
1 teaspoon dried garlic
1 teaspoon dried oregano
1 teaspoon dried basil
1 teaspoon dried thyme
1 teaspoon dried red pepper
¼ cup Parmesan cheese
4 whole wheat rolls, each sliced into 4 or 5 pieces

Mix olive oil, spices, and Parmesan cheese together and spread on top of the roll slices. Place on a baking sheet and bake for 10 minutes in a 425-degree oven. Makes 16–20 crostini.

NAVAJO FRY BREAD

2 cups whole wheat flour
½ teaspoon salt
1 tablespoon baking powder
¼ cup dry milk
¾ to 1 ½ cups warm water
3 to 4 cups shortening

In a bowl, mix dry ingredients. Add enough warm water to make a smooth, soft dough. Divide dough into four pieces and roll each into flat 9 inch circle. Break a small hole in the middle. In a large pan over high heat, melt shortening. Fry the dough until golden brown, turning once during cooking. Drain the fry bread on paper towels. Makes 4 fry breads.

OLIVE BREAD

2 ¼ cups whole wheat flour
2 tablespoons baking powder
1 teaspoon dried rosemary
½ teaspoon salt
2 tablespoons dry egg mix
⅓ cup dry milk
1 cup water
¼ cup olive oil
⅓ cup finely chopped walnuts
½ cup imported olives, seeded and chopped

In a large bowl, mix together the flour, baking powder, rosemary, salt, egg mix and dry milk. Add water and oil. Pour wet ingredients into dry. Turn with a spoon until the dry ingredients are just moistened. Add walnuts and olives. Fold in until evenly distributed. The batter will be stiff. Scrape into a greased, 6-cup loaf pan. Bake in a preheated 350-degree oven for 45 minutes. Cool on a rack 10 minutes and un-mold. Place on rack to completely cool. Makes 4–6 servings.

WHOLE WHEAT ROLLS/BREAD

2 cups water
⅔ cup dry milk
½ cup sugar
2 teaspoons salt
½ cup shortening
½ cup warm water
2 tablespoons active dry yeast
1 teaspoon sugar
7 cups whole wheat flour
2 tablespoons dry egg mix + 2 tablespoons water

In a pot on the stove, heat the water and mix in the dry milk. Scald. Add sugar, salt and shortening. Mix well. Let sit until cool.

Whisk warm water, yeast and sugar in a bowl until foamy. Let sit for 5 minutes. Add cooled milk mixture. Add flour. Mix until just blended. In a small dish, mix dry egg mix and water. Add to dough. Mix and knead well, 6 to 7 minutes, until dough is smooth and elastic. Place dough into a large greased bowl and turn to coat both sides. Cover with plastic wrap. Let rise until double. Punch down and divide in two. Place one half into a greased bread pan. Let rise again until doubled. Bake the loaf at 375 degrees for 25 minutes. Divide the other half into 8 pieces. Roll into balls, flatten a little and place 2 inches apart on a baking sheet. Let rise again until doubled. Bake at 375 degrees for 15 minutes. Makes 8 rolls or 1 loaf.

CORN TORTILLAS

2 cups masa harina
1 ¼ to 1 ⅓ cups hot water

Mix masa harina and water together by hand, adjusting the amount of water to make a soft dough, not too dry or too sticky. Cover with plastic and let rest 30 minutes. Knead the dough until it is pliable. Break off a piece and roll it into a 1 ½ inch ball. Cover remaining dough with plastic to keep it from drying out. Place in a 5 inch tortilla press until uniformly 1/16 inch thick. Place on preheated griddle 20seconds. Flip over to other side and cook 30 seconds. Flip again and cook 30 seconds. Remove to a clean towel and cover. Form and cook remaining dough the same way. Stack tortillas and cover. Makes 12 tortillas.

WHOLE WHEAT TORTILLAS

3 cups whole wheat flour
1 tablespoon baking powder
⅓ cup shortening
1 teaspoon salt
1 cup warm water
Additional flour

Mix flour, baking powder, shortening and salt together in a bowl. Rub the mixture together with your fingers until it forms small crumbs. Add the warm water and mix with a fork. Add some additional flour and knead by hand for a few minutes until the dough is smooth. Divide the dough into 12 balls, set them on a plate, cover with plastic wrap and let sit for 30 minutes.

On a lightly floured surface, with a rolling pin, roll out each ball into a paper thin circle. Bake on a very hot un-greased griddle until lightly freckled, about 30 seconds per side. Makes about 12 medium-size tortillas.

DANISH APPLESAUCE

2 cups water
2 cups dried apples
¼ cup sugar
2 tablespoons vanilla

Boil water in a pot, add the apple slices. Continue to boil for 5 minutes. Turn down heat to medium. Add sugar and vanilla. Use a potato masher to mash the apples into small chunks.

Turn down heat and simmer for 20 minutes. Add a little water if the sauce gets too dry. Makes 4–6 servings.

HARDTACK

⅓ cup dry milk + 1 ¼ cups warm water
3 cups quick oatmeal
1 cup oat bran
¾ cup sugar
1 ½ cups whole wheat flour
4 teaspoons baking powder
½ teaspoon salt

Whisk the dry milk and warm water together in a bowl. Soak the oatmeal and bran in the milk for 8 hours. Then add the sugar, flour, baking powder and salt. Mix and form into dough. Add more milk if too dry. Roll out on a baking sheet until very thin, less than ½ inch. Prick all over with a fork and cut into small squares with a pizza cutter or knife. Bake 10 to 15 minutes in a 400-degree oven. Done when browned to a light tan color. Cool and package in a cloth bag so it can dry out and last forever! Makes 48 2-inch squares.

HASH BROWN POTATOES

> 1 tablespoon dried onions
> 1 tablespoon dried green pepper (optional)
> ½ cup water
> 1 cup dried shredded or diced potatoes
> 3 cups boiling water
> 1 teaspoon salt
> 4 tablespoons butter-flavored shortening

In a small dish, rehydrate onions and green pepper, if using, I ½ cup water for 15 minutes then drain.

Pour dried potatoes into a pot of salted boiling water. Turn down heat and simmer until potatoes are tender, approximately 15 minutes. Drain and pat dry. Mix onions and green pepper with potatoes. Melt in a pan or on a griddle and add potato mixture, flattening evenly. Cook over medium heat until browned, then carefully flip over with a spatula and brown the other side. Makes 4 servings.

MASHED POTATOES

> 2 cups hot water
> 1 cup instant potato flakes
> 1 tablespoon dried sour cream mix
> 1 tablespoon dried cheese sauce mix
> ½ teaspoon dried garlic
> 1 tablespoon dried parsley

In a pot, bring water almost to a boil and then remove from heat. Add instant potato flakes and stir until thickened. Stir in sour cream, cheese, garlic and parsley. Makes 4 servings.

PORK FRIED RICE

¼ cup dried carrots
¼ cup dried peas
¼ cup dried green onions
1 cup water
2 tablespoons dry egg mix + 2 tablespoons water
1 can (15 ounces) pork chunks, drained
1 envelope (¾ounce) fried rice seasoning mix
½ cup olive oil
4 cups cold, cooked rice (see recipe page 116)
2 tablespoons soy sauce
½ teaspoon salt
½ teaspoon black pepper

Rehydrate carrots, peas and green onions in 1 cup of water for 15 minutes. Drain.

Set aside. Mix dried egg mix and water together. Heat oil in a wok pan and stir fry pork for 2 minutes, lightly browning. Add the egg mixture and scramble well. Add seasoning mix, rice, soy sauce, salt and pepper constantly stirring until hot and well mixed. Add carrots, peas and onions and continue to stir fry 3 minutes. Makes 4–6 servings.

RICE

2 cups white rice
4 cups water
2 teaspoons salt
6 cubes vegetable bouillon

Put rice, water, bouillon and salt into a pot and cover. Bring to a boil, then turn down heat and let simmer for 15 minutes. Makes 4 cups.

SPANISH RICE

1 cup white rice
2 cups water
1 teaspoon salt
1 cup salsa (see recipe page 117)

Put rice, water, and salt into a pot and cover. Bring to a boil, then turn down heat and let simmer for 15 minutes. Stir in salsa to taste. Makes 4 servings.

Refried Beans

    2 cups refried bean flakes
    2 cups boiling water
    1 can (4 ounces) green chiles
    1 teaspoon dried onions
    ½ teaspoon dried jalapenos (optional)

Stir refried bean flakes into boiling water. Lower heat and mix well. Add green chiles, onions and jalapenos. Cook on low heat for 5 minutes or until thickened. Makes 4 servings.

Salsa

    1 can (15 ounces) diced tomatoes
    1 tablespoon dried crushed lime
    ½ teaspoon granulated garlic
    1 tablespoon dried onions
    1 tablespoon dried cilantro
    ½ teaspoon dried jalapeno pepper
    ⅛ teaspoon cumin
    ½ teaspoon salt

Mix all ingredients together in an electric or hand-cranked food processor. Pulse 4 to 6 times. Correct seasoning to taste. Let stand 15 minutes. Makes 2 cups.

STUFFING

    ½ cup dried onions
    ½ cup dried celery
    1 cup water
    ½ cup butter-flavored shortening
    8 cubes chicken bouillon
    ½ teaspoon rubbed sage
    8 slices whole wheat toast, diced
    1 cup water, plus more if necessary

Soak onions and celery in water for 15 minutes. Drain well. Put shortening in a pot on high heat and add vegetables, sauté for 2 minutes. Lower heat to medium. Add the chicken bouillon and sage. Mix well. Add diced pieces of toast. Stir well. Add water slowly until it gets to the right consistency. Makes 4 servings.

WILD RICE CAKES

¼ cup dried onions
1 cup water
1 package (16 ounces) cooked wild rice
3 tablespoons whole wheat flour
1 ½ tablespoons baking powder
1 tablespoon salt
3 tablespoons dry egg mix + 3 tablespoons water
3 teaspoons dried ginger
2 teaspoons dried jalapenos (optional)
½ cup olive oil

Rehydrate onions in 1 cup water for 15 minutes. Drain.

In a large bowl, combine wild rice, flour, baking powder and salt. Mix well. In another bowl, whisk egg mixture, onions, ginger and jalapenos, if using. Add to rice mixture and blend together well.

In a large pan over high heat, add oil. Spoon mixture in 2 tablespoon-sized dollops into the pan. Shape into a cake with the spoon and cook until golden brown. Carefully turn over and cook the other side until browned. Transfer to paper towels then serve. Makes 12 cakes.

Dessert

Apple Crisp

Brownies

Cherry Cobbler

Chocolate Chip Pudding

Rice Pudding

Vanilla Berry Pudding

Whole Grain Chocolate Chip Pecan Cookies

Peach Cobbler

Peach Crumble

APPLE CRISP

> 2 cups water
> 4 cups dried apple slices
> ½ cup whole wheat flour
> 1 cup regular rolled oats
> ¾ cup packed brown sugar
> 1 teaspoon cinnamon
> ½ cup butter-flavored shortening
> ½ cup chopped walnuts(optional)

Preheat the oven to 375 degrees. Boil water in a pot. Place the apple slices into an 8 x 8-inch baking dish. Pour the boiling water over the apples and let them sit while mixing the topping. Combine the remaining ingredients with a large fork until it gets crumbly. Sprinkle the topping evenly over the apples. Tap the baking dish to settle the crumbs. Bake 45 to 55 minutes, until topping is golden brown. Makes 4 to 6 servings.

BROWNIES

4 ounces unsweetened chocolate, chopped
½ cup butter-flavored shortening
2 cups sugar
2 teaspoons vanilla
4 tablespoons dry egg mix + 4 tablespoons water
1 cup whole wheat flour
1 cup chopped walnuts/pecans (optional)

In a pot on the stove, over very low heat, melt chocolate and butter shortening stirring constantly until smooth. Cool completely. Add sugar and vanilla. Stir until well combined.

In a small dish, mix dry egg mix and water. Add to pot and continue to stir. Add flour and nuts. Stir until just combined. Preheat oven to 350 degrees. Pour batter into a greased 8-inch baking dish. Bake 25 minutes or until a toothpick comes out clean. Cool completely. Cut into four squares. Makes 4 servings.

CHERRY COBBLER

   1 cup whole wheat flour
   ¾ cup sugar
1 ½ teaspoons baking powder
   ¼ teaspoon salt
   ½ cup butter-flavored shortening
   1 can (28 ounces) cherry pie filling

Mix flour, sugar, baking powder and salt in a bowl. Cut in shortening with a pastry blender or 2 knives until the mixture resembles coarse crumbs. Pour the cherry pie filling into an 8 x 8-inch baking dish and top with the flour mixture. Bake in a preheated 350-degree oven for 30minutes or until the topping turns golden brown. Cool and serve. Makes 4 to 6 servings.

CHOCOLATE CHIP PUDDING

1 ½ cups chocolate pudding mix or boxed pudding mix
2 ⅔ cups water
  ¼ cup white chocolate chips
  ¼ cup semi sweet chocolate chips

Blend pudding mix and water until smooth. If using boxed pud- ding mix, follow package directions. Stir in chocolate chips then chill 15 minutes. Makes 4 servings.

RICE PUDDING

1 ½ cups water
¼ teaspoon salt
¾ cup medium or long-grain rice
4 cups warm water
1 ⅓ cups dry milk
½ cup sugar
½ teaspoon vanilla
Ground cinnamon

In a pot over medium heat, bring water, salt and rice to a simmer. Reduce heat to low, cover and cook until the water is absorbed, about 15 minutes. In a bowl, whisk together warm water, dry milk and sugar. Stir milk mixture into pot. Cook, uncovered, over medium heat until the mixture thickens, about 35 minutes. Stir in vanilla. Pour into a large bowl (or four individual dishes) and press plastic wrap over the surface to prevent a skin from forming. Serve warm or cold. Sprinkle ground cinnamon on top. Makes 4 servings.

VANILLA BERRY PUDDING

    1 cup vanilla pudding mix or boxed pudding mix
    2 cups water
    ½ cup dried berry mix (strawberry, raspberry, blueberry)

Blend pudding mix and water until smooth. If using boxed pudding mix, follow package directions. Stir in the berry mix and chill. Makes 4 servings.

WHOLE GRAIN CHOCOLATE CHIP PECAN COOKIES

1 cup butter-flavored shortening
1 cup sugar
1 cup brown sugar
4 tablespoons dry egg mix + ¾ cup water
2 teaspoons vanilla
2 cups whole wheat flour
2 cups quick oatmeal, blended into flour
1 cup oat bran
½ teaspoon salt
2 teaspoons baking soda
2 teaspoons baking powder
2 cups semisweet chocolate chips
2 cups finely chopped pecans

In a large bowl, cream shortening and sugars together. In a small bowl, whisk dry eggs and water. Add eggs and vanilla to creamed shortening and sugars. In another bowl, mix flour, oatmeal, oat bran, salt, baking soda, baking powder, chocolate chips and pecans. Add liquid to dry ingredients. Mix well. Roll into small balls and flatten a little. Place on baking sheets and bake for exactly 10 minutes in a preheated 375- degree oven. Cool on a wire rack. Makes approximately 4 dozen cookies.

PEACH COBBLER

        1 cup whole wheat flour
        ¾ cup sugar
    1 ½ teaspoons baking powder
        ¼ teaspoon salt
½ cup butter-flavored shortening
    1 can (28 ounces) peach pie filling

In a bowl, mix together flour, sugar, baking powder and salt. Cut in shortening with a pastry blender or 2 knives until the mixture resembles coarse crumbs. Pour the peach pie filling into an 8 x 8-inch baking dish and top with the flour mixture. Bake in a preheated 350-degree oven for 30 minutes or until the topping turns golden brown. Cool and serve. Makes 4 to 6 servings.

PEACH CRUMBLE

2 cups boiling water
4 cups dried peach flakes
½ cup whole wheat flour
1 cup regular rolled oats
¾ cup packed brown sugar
1 teaspoon cinnamon
½ cup butter-flavored shortening
½ cup chopped almonds (optional)

Preheat the oven to 375 degrees. Boil water in a pot. Place the peach flakes into an 8 x 8-inch baking dish. Pour the boiling water over the peaches and let them sit while mixing the topping. Combine the remaining ingredients with a large fork until it gets crumbly. Sprinkle the topping evenly over the peaches. Tap the baking dish to settle the crumbs. Bake 45 to 55 minutes, until topping is golden brown. Makes 4 to 6 servings.

Other Important Storage Components

WATER

Potable water is one of the most important elements of survival. We just can't live without it. With it freely flowing from our taps, we don't often worry about storing it. However, for the residents of Phoenix, Arizona, affected by the "boil order" at the end of January 2005, there was cause for concern. All gallon bottles of water in most stores were gone within 2 hours of the early morning "boil order" announcement. If you were prepared with water storage, you were secure and unaffected by this incident that lasted three days.

Water storage can be practical and convenient to do. Just like food storage, it must always be used and rotated continuously. There are several ways to store water in many different containers: water tanks, 55-gallon drums, 5-gallon water bottles, 2 ½-gallon containers, 1-gallon bottles, and cases of bottled water in all shapes and sizes, etc.

The 55-gallon drum can be inconvenient to use on a regular basis. Some people who store water this way just empty and refill the drum once a year instead of using it. It is also practically impossible to carry if you have to evacuate your home. The 2 ½ and 1 gallon water bottles sold in food stores are made of thin plastic that is biodegradable so they do not store well and tend to leak after a few months.

The container that is the most efficiently rotated is the portable and durable 5-gallon water bottle when used with a water cooler, because it is in constant use. Many people have drinking water delivered to them by companies and receive the cooler free. If a company is used for water delivery, purchase several extra 5 gallon bottles of your own to rotate with the company bottles. Empty 5 gallon bottles with handles can be purchased for under $7.00. Hot/cold water coolers are available for around $100.00. Most water stores refill the 5-gallon bottles for $1.25. How much water should be stored? Two weeks of drinking water should always be on hand. Simply calculate the number of people in the household by one gallon of water per day to find out how many 5 gallon water bottles are needed for two weeks' storage of portable, potable drinking water. For example: 4 people x 1 gallon = 4 gallons per day x 14 days = 56 gallons divided by 5 = 11 five gallon water bottles needed.

There are many beverages that can be stored depending upon individual tastes, but always store water first. Dried drink mixes and powders have a longer shelf-life than bottled drinks and don't take up as much room for storage.

If you have babies or small children, be sure to store extra dry milk for drinking.

SPROUTING AND GARDENING

Sprouting is an invaluable addition to a food storage diet. It may be the only fresh food available to you for an indefinite period. It is said that there is more nutrition packed into a plant's sprout than in the mature plant at harvest.

If you were to start one tablespoon of sprouting seeds every three days, you would have a constant supply of fresh sprouts on hand. There are many different varieties of sprouting seeds available: alfalfa, broccoli, radish, mung bean, pea, sunflower, salad mixes with several different kinds of seeds, wheat, oats, rye, etc. Several different sprouting trays are available on the market, but a wide-mouthed quart jar will work just fine. Fill the jar about ¾ full with water. Add the seed sand soak them for 8 to 12 hours. Cover the top of the jar with a piece of nylon, mesh, or screen fabric and secure it with the lid ring or a rubber band. Pour the water out and set the jar on its side in a dark place. Three times a day, fill the jar with water and immediately pour it off, shaking gently. Some seeds do have specific instructions, so check the package. In addition to being a sandwich filler or salad, sprouts can be mixed into most soups, stews, and casseroles. Wheat, oats or rye sprouts can also be added to bread dough for extra nutrition.

Home gardening is an excellent source of food for storage. It provides the freshest foods to be canned or dehydrated for storage. Take advantage of producing your own food from a garden. If space is a problem, use pots. There are many books and publications on gardening in your area and climate. For local information, check with your own State University's Cooperative Extension Service.

ALL THAT OTHER STUFF

How does one figure out how much toilet paper to store for a year? It is easy to calculate the average number of rolls of toilet paper or any other non-perishable item, if you get in the habit of marking the date of purchase on everything you buy. This is a good habit, because you need to use it again when you open that 30-roll package of toilet paper on your storage shelf and mark on it the date you begin to use it. Then, when it is all gone, note the date you finished it and see how long it took your family to go through 30 rolls of toilet paper. If it was two and a half months, divide 12 by 2.5 and get 4.8. So, you need five 30-roll packages of toilet paper for a year's supply. Do that with everything from toothpaste to laundry soap!

Remember to consider First Aid supplies and personal medicines in your storage plan .Also, have enough clothing and bedding in your home to accommodate your family for an extended period of time. It is handy to have sewing supplies such as fabric, thread and needles to make repairs. Of course, don't forget a reserve of fuel (coal, charcoal, wood and oil)for cooking and some heating. (Be aware that storing some fuels can be dangerous and is prohibited by law in some places.) Candles, batteries, and oil lamps are also important items to have on hand.

THE SNACK PACK

The "Snack Pack" is simply a small- to medium-size backpack (a castoff from last school year will do) that is filled with healthy and ready-to-eat snacks and drinks. This convenient pack should be used ALL of the time. It is not meant to filled and forgotten in some closet. Take it out with you all of the time, use it and replenish it. Toss it in the car every time you leave home. In the heat of the summer, place it in a cooler in your vehicle. It will satisfy hungry children and save money by making stops at fast food restaurants and gas station stores no longer necessary. By using it all of the time, it will always be stocked with fresh food and available at a moment's notice to provide your family with food in any emergency situation.

Below are some examples of items that could be included in your snack pack

◊ backpack

◊ can opener

◊ plastic utensils

◊ napkins or wet wipes

◊ granola bars

◊ protein bars

◊ canned pasta

◊ canned chicken lunches
  (with crackers)

◊ canned tuna (with crackers)

◊ canned Vienna sausage

◊ beef jerky

◊ turkey jerky

◊ salmon jerky

◊ Slim Jims

◊ crackers

◊ cheese/peanut butter crackers

◊ pretzels

◊ chips

◊ mini rice cakes

◊ nuts

◊ sunflower seeds

◊ trail mix

◊ cereal breakfast bars

◊ Pop Tarts

◊ dried fruits

◊ fruit cocktail or fruit cups

◊ fruit snacks or fruit roll ups

◊ applesauce cups

◊ raisins

◊ juice boxes

◊ energy drinks

◊ V-8 juice

◊ Snickers bars

◊ hard candy

◊ licorice

THE 72-HOUR SURVIVAL KIT

According to the American Red Cross, "it is very important for each family to have an accessible kit that would help sustain life for up to 3 days if needed. It is said that local governments and cities often need 3 days to get basic utilities back on line in times of disaster." In other words, you can really be on your own for 72 hours. Most search and rescue operations are called off after 3 days because most people are unprepared and usually don't survive beyond that time frame.

FEMA's publication, *Are You Ready? A Guide to Citizen Preparedness* includes information on how to prepare for a disaster whether natural, technological, or man-made. Do you know what to do if there is an incident at the nuclear power plant? Can you leave your home in 10 minutes time with what it takes to survive for 3 days? For a free copy of this publication call FEMA's Distribution Center at 1-800- 480-2520 or visit FEMA online at www.fema.gov/library.

Everyone needs a 72-hour kit and the skills to use it. Many families already have one. There are numerous versions of kits, from one that fits in a fanny pack to large backpacks or duffle bags that include tents and sleeping bags.

A good example of a 72-hour kit is can be found in the book, *98.6 Degrees: The Art of Keeping Your Ass Alive* (Gibbs Smith, Publisher, 2003), by Cody Lundine. The author goes into great detail on how to survive fear, panic, and the biggest outdoor killers. He also explains why several of his 72-hour survival kit components are important and how to use them. He teaches that food is not necessary in the kit, as most adults can usually go 3 days without food and with little discomfort. However, as I discussed with him at a survival class he taught a few years ago, when you have hungry children with you, they will multiply the stress level tenfold! So, I developed the "Snack Pack to complement the 72-hour survival kit.

AUTHOR'S REMARKS

It is my sincere hope that something in this book will spark your imagination and inspire you to start a food storage plan in your home, or revitalize the storage you already have in place.

Resources

FRESH, WHOLE GRAINS:

Bob's Red Mill
800-553-2258
www.bobsredmill.com

Eden Foods
888-441-3336
www.edenfoods.com

Great River Organic Milling
608-687-9580
www.greatrivermilling.com

Montana Milling
800-548-8554
www.montanamilling.com

Sun Organic Farm
888-269-9888
www.sunorganicfarm.com

GRAIN MILLS:

Bosch (Nutrimill, Ultra Mill)
800-692-6724
www.boschmixers.com

Country Living Productions, Inc.
360-652-0671
www.countrylivinggrainmills.com

Lehman's (Diamant)
888-438-5346
www.lehmans.com

Pleasant Hill Grain (Nutrimill)
800-321-1073
www.pleasanthillgrain.com

Retsel (Grain Master Whisper Mill, Mill-Rite)
(011) 61-3-9795-2725
www.retsel.com.au
(The Mill-Rite can be both electric and manual.)

Vita-mix
800-848-2649
www.vitamix.com

PRODUCTS AND INFORMATION:

Emergency Essentials
800-999-1863
www.beprepared.com
Large selection of emergency and storage supplies

FEMA
800-480-2520
www.fema.gov
Free emergency books and information

Fresh Preserving
www.freshpreserving.com
Information on how-to canning basics, recipes and products

The Mesa Cannery
480-967-8551
This Dry & Wet Pack Facility has canning supplies and bulk or canned dried foods: dried apple slices; black, pinto, refried flakes and white beans; dried carrots, flour, fruit drink mix, hot cocoa mix, macaroni, dry milk, regular rolled oats, quick oats, dried onions, instant potato pearls (instant potatoes) chocolate and vanilla pudding mixes, white rice, spaghetti, hard red wheat and hard white wheat. Also salt (2-packs of shakers) and plain shortening (in 3-pound cans) are available.

Lodge Cast Iron
423-837-7171
www.lodgemfg.com
Large selection of cast-iron cookware including the Camp Dutch ovens in many sizes, cast-iron griddles, books and videos

Suns Ovens International
800-408-7919
Easy to use, portable solar oven with locking glass lid and thermostat

Index

CPSIA information can be obtained
at www.ICGtesting.com
Printed in the USA
FSHW020720270320

9 781423 656760